Activities for PE

USING SMALL APPARATUS

John Severs

BLACKWELL EDUCATION

First published 1991

Published by
Basil Blackwell Ltd
108 Cowley Road
Oxford OX4 1JF

British Library Cataloguing in Publication Data
Severs, John
    Activities for P. E. using small apparatus.
    1. Primary schools. Curriculum. Physical education.
    Teaching
    I. Title
    372.86044

    ISBN 0-631-17943-7

Illustrations by Jane Bottomley
Typeset in 12 pt Palatino
by Best-Set Typesetter Ltd, Hong Kong
Printed in Great Britain by Dotesios Ltd, Trowbridge

The author would like to thank the pupils of Birtley East Primary School (Gateshead LEA) for their help during the writing of this book.

Contents

Introduction

This book is intended for all teachers and students who would like to sample, or develop to the full, the activity potential offered by the full range of 'small apparatus', namely beanbags, balls of different types and sizes, hoops, ropes, bats and quoits.

This apparatus offers marvellous opportunities in respect of both range of skill and diversity, with material covering gymnastic activities particularly of the basic movement type (jumping, rolling, off the hands etc); static and dynamic balance; transporting; passing and moving objects; throwing; catching; dribbling and hitting; activities specific to a given piece and, finally, a number of simple competitions.

The activities are particularly suitable for primary school children and many can be attempted by reception and even nursery children. Much of the material can also be of value to upper middle and lower secondary school pupils. Here it can be used either to add variety to the programme or, specifically, to improve basic skills (eg, in catching and throwing) which may be currently lacking, and thus contribute to building a solid platform upon which the more advanced games orientated skills are based.

As average ability and range of skill will vary from class to class with maturation levels, innate ability and, particularly, past experience, no attempt has been made to specify at what age a given activity should be attempted. However, within a particular section practices are listed in order of difficulty, allowing the teacher to choose or experiment according to the needs of their own pupils.

It is vitally important that children are not asked to attempt activities until they have the capacity to succeed in them. If no progress is made the experience may produce immediate negative responses and, if repeated in other spheres, frustration could possibly lead to a long term disinclination to work hard and achieve improvement. The wide range of activities offered here with, in many cases, varied opportunities for working at different skill levels can ensure – with careful selection – that all children will gain satisfaction through achievement.

Although the book is of a practical nature, concerned with lesson content and not with curriculum development, it is nevertheless important that the teacher should know how the material can best be used. To this effect 'back-up' sections on lesson form, including mixed activity groupwork, progression, teaching strategies, organisation of equipment and pupils, safe practice, evaluation and suggestions on time allocation have been included.

The appendices give information on how to develop or organise certain types of activity which apply to more than one piece of apparatus, and on which equipment to stock.

The first set of activities provide new dimensions for work on basic body control, adding both variety and purpose to movement and balance. Attention can be sustained for longer periods allowing more useful practice to take place. This leads, for example in Activity 1, to improved awareness of the different parts of the body, the different directions and the variety of shapes that can be employed in moving. Improved control should also result from the varied and repeated practice.

1 Moving over a beanbag

This type of activity is particularly valuable for reception and infant children.

One beanbag per child spaced evenly over the hall floor or playground area being used.

a Jumping
- Forwards

- Sideways and backwards; diagonally

- With varying degrees of twist

- To adopt different shapes both in the air and on landing

- All the above aiming to hold the landing position absolutely still

- For distance – toes up to the bag, jump as far as possible. Stop. Turn round and use the bag as a target to clear

- Hopping

- Combinations of some of the above (eg sideways and small body)

b Hands and feet
- As above varying direction, shape and height

- Aiming to lift the seat and/or feet as high as possible ('How close to the ceiling or the sky can you get your foot or feet?')

- Aiming to straighten the legs during the movement

- Using just one foot or one hand on the ground

c Other body parts
Using parts such as knees, tummy, forearms etc to move on
or to move onto.

2 Moving over two beanbags
Two beanbags are used as an easily adjusted target to move
over. Two pupils of similar ability work together aiming to
increase the distance between the bags so that it becomes a
real challenge to move across without touching them.
Movements may be

a jumping and hopping; forward, sideways etc, from
standing, with one step, with a short run etc.

b where contact is made with the floor in between with the
hands as in a bunny jump or cartwheel.

3 Moving in and out of beanbags
*This activity encourages imagination both from the
pupils and the teacher in stimulating less capable
children.*

Four beanbags are placed in a straight or curved line, say 1
metre apart. The children find ways of moving in and out of
the bags, in some cases copying each other.

·　·　·　·

*While clearly designed to help develop static and dynamic
balancing ability, the following activities, in encouraging
the use of a wide range of body parts, also lead to
enhancement of pupil knowledge (names of body parts
and uses).*

4 Touching the beanbag
Again particularly valuable for reception/infant.

a While maintaining contact with the floor with foot or feet,
touch the beanbag in order of progression of difficulty with

- toe; heel; instep; side of foot
- finger; hand; wrist; elbow; shoulder
- forehead; nose; chin
- knee

b Balancing on other parts of the body (eg knees, hands and
feet/foot, seat), touch the beanbag with parts as above if
appropriate or, if possible, with tummy, chest, hip or ear.

5 Balancing on a beanbag

With or, more normally, without other body parts touching the floor balance on the beanbag using

- the soles of the feet; toes; heels; one foot
- tummy; seat; hip
- knees; one knee
- shoulders, normally with the hands supporting the hips

6 Balancing the beanbag on parts of the body

a While maintaining a static position on two feet and later on one foot, the seat and so on, the beanbag may be balanced on

- the hand – palm, knuckles, back, side
- wrist, forearm, upper arm, top of each shoulder
- chest, back of the neck, upper back
- head – top, forehead
- the top of the foot while on the ground or lifted
- the thigh, knee, back of the heel

b Changing shape or position while remaining on the spot.

For example a child standing upright balances a beanbag on top of his/her head. The child then aims to sit down. Depending on the age/skill level of the children difficulty may be increased by, for example, not allowing the hands any contact with the floor, having to lift both feet off the floor as soon as the seat is in position, or getting as close to lying down as possible.

Alternatively, while the child is sitting down the bag may be placed on one or two feet and lifted off the ground. Difficulty may be increased by aiming to lift the foot/feet as high as possible or maintaining the position as still as possible.

c Moving across the floor in different directions, with the bag balanced on parts as above

- in a simple way, eg sliding the feet or walking
- involving other parts of the body, eg moving across the floor on hands and feet; sliding or spinning on the seat or tummy
- in ways demanding a high level of skill, such as hopping or two foot jumping. Success may be measured by achieving a target, eg five hops without losing the bag.

Movements in a backwards direction should be of the slow, controlled type or a single phase, plus a definite stop such as a short double foot jump. Running, hopping and jumping backward continuously should be avoided because of the danger of falling backwards or colliding with others.

7 Beanbags as aids in gymnastic apparatus balance work

These activities not only add a new dimension in terms of the range, difficulty and therefore challenge of balance work available to the children, but create enormous interest and are very enjoyable.

For these activities use a bench rib (ie upside down) or a balance bar – about 30/40 cms from the floor – for the majority of juniors or top infants and the bench top itself for lower infants and those at lower levels who have poor dynamic balance or are incapable of working on a narrow surface.

a Slide the feet or walk along the bar/bench, possibly in different directions, with the beanbag balanced on different parts of the body (see **6** above).

b While standing on the rib etc bend down to pick up a bag from the floor. The bag may also be passed between the rib/bar and the bench top/floor.

c Place the beanbag on the bench top or rib. Aim to touch it with different body parts while remaining balanced. There should be no contact with the floor.

For toe, heel, finger, elbow etc, balance is maintained on the feet/foot. Later it is possible to 'drop' onto one knee (with the foot) and this in turn, possibly with hand(s) on the rib, enables contact to be made by the nose – by a gifted few.

d Change shape or position, eg moving onto different body parts on the rib while balancing a bag on a variety of body parts.

e Throw and catch in pairs. **A** stands on or walks along the bench rib, while **B** stands on the floor one metre from the end of the bench.

With imaginative planning the activities described above may be developed in parallel or integrated with 'pure' gymnastics work being done on floor and apparatus.

8 Trapping the beanbag between parts of the body

Individually
The beanbag is held between different parts of the body
either while holding still or moving. The easiest – suitable for
reception children – are between the hand and, say, the head,
shoulder or hip. The 'same' parts may also be used, for
example between the wrists, forearms, thighs, calves and feet
(*see relays*).

With partners
A more interesting development, again done in static
positions or travelling. The bag may be held between the
shoulders (side), upper backs, hips, seats, wrists, foreheads,
ankles and the sides or soles of the feet.

9 Passing the beanbag
*These activities are principally for fun but also require a
high degree of control in moving the object while
maintaining balance.*

Individually
i Using the hands while standing. Pass the bag from hand to
hand **a** though the legs **b** round the neck **c** round the back
of the legs **d** under one leg while balanced on the other and
e over the shoulder to the other hand behind the back, right
to left and vice versa.

**ii Using the hands while sitting, knees raised and slightly
apart, the feet on or off the floor.** As above except for **d**.

iii Using the foot while standing or sitting. Lift up to the
hand.

With partners
Standing and possibly sitting, kneeling or crouching, pass the
beanbag

i Round the back. Facing partner, **A** passes right (RT) to left
(LT) behind his/her own back, from LT into **B**'s RT, **B** passes
RT to LT behind the back and finally back into **A**'s RT.
Alternatively a figure of 8 pattern may be used.

ii Round the neck, back of the legs etc. Partners can face
each other, face the same direction or work side by side.

iii Back to back. Pass over the head and back through the
legs.

10 Throwing

The use of a beanbag for throwing lays down an excellent foundation for later activities. Even reception children can attempt the simpler close range activities: because the bag doesn't roll away like a ball the pupils are often able to note how effective a throw has been and many more attempts can be made in a given time span. Another advantage is that the children do not have to continually run in and out of each other to retrieve the object after it has been thrown. The wide range of activities possible enables rapid improvement to be made in judging the forces and angles required; for distance – underarm, sidearm and overarm – and for accuracy and direction.

• Throw over a rope placed on the ground starting at close range and gradually extending the distance

• Throw up to varying heights to land near the feet in front, to the side and behind the body

• As for preceding exercise but aim to land in hoops placed near the feet and later, at different distances and angles

• Into bins or baskets, normally upright but possibly lying on their sides

• Through hoops placed at an angle to a wall or on top of skittles

• Between cones, domes or skittles placed at varying distances apart and from the thrower

• To hit a suspended braid or to pass through a suspended hoop

• To hit or knock down an object, eg a skittle

• Over a net or suspended rope to land in marked areas or hoops

• Between canes or ropes fixed in parallel to posts

Research has shown that reception and early infant children cannot normally profit from practice aimed at improving distance throwing or catching. Depending on maturation, children should be around six or seven before this type of activity is attempted. Otherwise, as stated in the introduction, frustration and a disinclination to persevere may be the result. They can profit, however, from practice where the bag lands near to the thrower.

. . . .

The exercises outlined in the following three sections form a carefully controlled progression which, if matched to capability and given sufficient time for plenty of repetition, should lead children to develop real skill in accurate throwing and 'clean' catching.

The shape and texture of the beanbag make it possible to attempt many catching activities some considerable time before they could be successfully done with a ball. Catching work with a small ball thus becomes a progression from the work with the beanbag.

11 Throwing and catching individually
Stand firmly on the spot with one foot a foot's length in front of the other.

Catching may be done with **a** the sides of the hands and little fingers placed together, palms parallel to the floor and slightly cupped – a very open position or **b** with the heels of the hands placed together, fingers thrusting upwards and outwards, rather like an inverted bell – a more closed position.

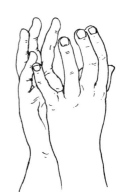

In each case, initially, the children should be encouraged to close the fingers round the bag and bring it to the chest as soon as a firm hold has been established. Practice should be started by throwing the bag just a few centimetres above head height until the technique has been established and the children are consistently successful. Subsequent activities could include

● throwing upwards accurately – start at one metre above the head, gradually increasing the height with each successful catch

i allowing both feet to move

ii movement of one foot in any direction

iii both feet to remain anchored

● throwing whilst clapping – throw up, clap hands, catch. Aim to gradually increase the number of claps (1–3–5–7)

● touching different parts of the body before catching

Easy chest, tummy, head, shoulders, hips

Moderate back, back of neck, knees

Hard shins, calves, toes/floor

- catching the beanbag opposite different parts of the body

Easy chest, tummy, face

Moderate thighs

Hard knees, shins

Very hard ankles

- with movement or balances on the spot

i sit down or get onto knees before catching

ii jump to full stretch in the air to catch

- throwing from one hand to the other – in front of the body, over the head, under the leg and so on

- throwing the bag 2 or 3 metres ahead in an arc and run to catch it before it drops to the ground

- walking or jogging forwards or sideways while throwing and catching

All of the above and many of the following practices can be attempted with one hand, first using the preferred and then the non-preferred.

12 Throwing and catching with partners

Young infants can start about one metre apart. Partner **A** holds hands out, cupped and parallel to the floor. Partner **B** transfers the beanbag from his/her own hands, first by simply dropping it into **A**'s hands. **B** can then tip the bag in, pushing it forward off two hands and later, gradually moving further away, can begin to gently lob it across, using one hand to throw. When catching can be confidently undertaken at a distance of 3 or 4 metres then the following progression can be started. Pupils can be randomly spaced in pairs around the hall or playground or placed in lines, allowing space for limited backward movement.

a Throw and catch aiming for partner's chest/tummy area
Throw one handed, catch with two and as in the solo practices aim to bring the bag into the body in the early stages. With success the basic distance of around 3 to 4 metres can be extended, particularly on a playground or field where there is plenty of space.

b Throwing at different heights
- aiming for different parts of the body – difficulty increases as the bag is aimed lower.

- throwing the bag higher into the air.

c Competitions
- First pair to make 10 catches and sit or crouch down.

- *Beat the record.* This contest is better, as it allows all pairs to compete successfully. Each pair tries to make as many catches as possible in, say, 15 or 20 seconds. All scores are checked. The children then aim to beat their scores in a second attempt over the same time span. Normally about two thirds succeed in doing this.

d Stretching to catch
A throws to the left and right of **B**, gradually 'forcing' more movement across, until a step has to be taken and the catch is made with one hand at full stretch.

Stretching can also be done to all hourly 'clock' positions from 7 o'clock to 5 o'clock.

Jumping up at full stretch is possible for a limited range of clock positions, say 11–1.

e Moving to catch
- in a straight line – partners move to 5 metres apart and the bag is either thrown a little short so that one or two forward steps must be taken in order to catch it *or* a little long over the head so that one or two steps backwards must be taken. Distances between throwers may be reduced again for the latter.

- at angles – **A** throws to **B** and moves immediately to a new position at right angles to **B**, 3–4 metres away. **B** on catching the bag immediately turns to face **A**, throws and moves into a position at right angles to **A** and so on. Angles, distances and speed of movement can be varied.

f Tricks
A stands with his/her back to **B** and throws the bag over the head or through the legs. Many upper juniors can stand back to back and both throw and catch between the legs and a select few can manage it overhead.

g With two beanbags
Encourage either high and low or throwing right to left in order to avoid collisions.

13 Throwing and catching in groups

There is no advantage to be gained from working in large groups as the amount of contact experienced by each child is reduced in proportion to the numbers involved. However there is something to be gained from working in threes or fours as follows:

- Making a triangle or square formation and passing the beanbag round. The child changes direction between receiving and passing and must move the feet into a new position before throwing.

- 'Pepper Pot'

A throws, initially in order and then randomly, to **B**, **C** and **D** who return the ball to **A**.

14 Flicking

a The beanbag is placed on the top of one foot ('instep') and is 'flicked' to a partner standing a few metres away. Difficulty can be increased by using the non-preferred foot, extending the distance between the partners, aiming to land the beanbag in a hoop placed on the floor or passing it through hoops of different sizes held vertically by a partner.

b The beanbag is gripped between the feet and flicked up forwards or behind the body to be caught by self or partner.

15 Sliding

Beanbags can be slid indoors along smooth surfaces.

The beanbag is propelled out of the hand using a technique akin to bowls – knees bent, hand close to the floor on release – to slide it to a partner. Distances may be quite close at first, say 4 or 5 metres, but later the whole width of the hall can be used.

For accuracy the bag may have to pass between markers placed midway between the pairs or between a partner's legs, with the target gap reduced as skill increases. Scoring may be introduced with competitions of the 'beat the record' or 'pair total v. other pairs' variety, for example six to ten attempts, with a score of two points if the bag passes cleanly through the legs and one point if the foot is hit.

16 Competitions

a Balance and move
Example: place beanbag on the head – first to sit down – no hand contact with floor – and first to stand up again.

b Target type
i With partners. Each pair has a beanbag each and a hoop which is placed in line down the playground or at each side of the hall, leaving at least a metre between hoops. Both partners stand side by side facing the hoop, at least a metre away from it. Each throws, aiming to get the bag to land in the hoop. If successful they take a short step back, if not they throw again from the same spot. Continue for, say, ten throws to see how far away each child can get.

ii In pairs as part of groupwork (see Unit 7). Each pair, normally two, has a bin, basket or box and eight to ten bags either each or between them. Bags are thrown either alternately or one child after the other depending on availability of bags. Throws may be repeated from the same position to attempt a score improvement, with the opposite hand, from a greater distance, with a different type of throw and so on.

c Keep the kettle boiling
The teacher, standing in the centre of the playground or hall, throws the bags in different directions and different distances. The children pick up one bag at a time and run with it to the container. It must be dropped in, never thrown. The teacher tries to empty the bin while the children try to stop this happening. The children always win. This is an excellent way of starting or finishing an infant lesson.

d He
Pupils should be in pairs, ideally matched for speed. **A** moves away from **B** to the opposite end of the hall or playground. On the signal **B** with the beanbag, chases after **A** aiming to hit his/her legs, possibly below the knee. It is vitally important that the bag is released, that is, thrown and not simply touched on the leg. If the bag hits, **A** picks it up and pursues **B**; if not **B** picks it up and tries again.

Relays
Using beanbags is an ideal way to introduce young children to relays. For notes on organisation and numbers, see Appendix 2.

a Passing the beanbag

These activities can be performed in teams of three, or four at most.

- Sit one behind another in parallel lines, cross-legged on the floor. One or more bags are placed on the floor in front of the first team member. Each bag is *passed* back from hand to hand and finally dropped behind the last team member's head on to the floor or into a hoop. The first team to pass all the bags back to the end is the winner.

- Stand one behind another in parallel lines. The bag may be passed overhead, through the legs, from side to side or using combinations of these techniques.

b Sliding the beanbag

Stand two metres apart, middle team members with legs apart. The first in line aims to slide the bag back through his own legs and through the 'middle' legs to the team member at the rear. Middle children only touch the bag if it goes off course or stops short. The last in the line picks it up as soon as it arrives and runs to the front, the others shuffling back two metres. The process is repeated until all have run to the front and the original formation is back in line.

All the above can also be attempted while sitting or standing on or astride a bench.

c Throwing the beanbag

The children sit or stand 3 to 4 metres apart in lines. The beanbag may be moved down the line in two ways.

- All face the same direction and throw the bag back over the head, possibly looking over the shoulder to ensure accuracy

- Turning round each time the bag is received and throwing straight to the next child's chest.

In each case simple continuity can be maintained by all members turning round to face the opposite way when the beanbag reaches the end and throwing it back down the line again.

d Using the feet

The children sit with legs straight out in front, a body length apart. The first in line grips the beanbag between the feet and rocks back on to the shoulders. The legs are extended behind and beyond the body and the beanbag is dropped on to the floor.

Immediately the next in line grips it between the feet, rocking back so that the legs go beyond the head, and drops it. When the beanbag reaches the last in the line he/she stands up, grips it between the feet and using a double foot action jumps to the front of the line, sits down and starts the process again. The children may have to shuffle back each time if there is pressure on space.

e Catching versus running

Pupils are in matched blocks of six or eight divided into teams of three or four (fours illustrated below). Team **A, B, C, D** stands inside the markers, placed 10 to 15 metres apart. Standing anything from 3 to 6 metres apart they see how many catches can be taken, throwing the beanbag round the square while Team **1, 2, 3, 4** run one at a time round the markers, passing a beanbag on in place of a baton. The teams are then reversed, with the numbered group attempting to beat the lettered group's catching score.

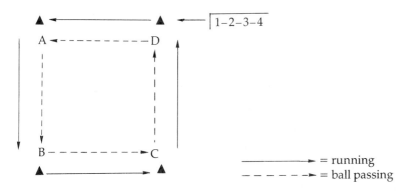

= running
= ball passing

What ball should be used?

Balls vary in terms of their make-up, weight and size. Suitability will not only depend on the maturation levels of the children and the skill being attempted, but also on levels of experience and where the practice is taking place – field, playground or indoors. The latter has safety implications that do not apply to the others.

*Balls available may be termed **large** (16–18cms), **medium** (11–14cms) and **small** (6–9cms with 7cms being tennis ball size). Medium and large balls may be made of sponge, uncoated or coated with a tougher material for outdoor use, or made of plastic of different thicknesses, often brightly coloured and usually inflatable. Small balls may be quite soft (sponge and hollow rubber), hard (composition or solid rubber) or in-between (soft solid rubber and tennis). Airflow or gamester balls, made from rigid tough plastic with sections cut out, may also be used. Although their bounce may not be as true as the others, flight is restricted by air resistance; consequently they are particularly useful for hitting activities played in a restricted area, and as protection indoors against windows or only partially protected lights.*

Young children, particularly reception and lower infants, will be much happier in the early stages carrying, rolling, steering, throwing, bouncing and balancing a brightly coloured medium sized ball than a dark, heavy small one. Task difficulty can be increased as part of skill progression by changing conditions such as distances and time limitations and by using a different ball; therefore older pupils may need a smaller ball, possibly of different texture, to be properly challenged in a given practice. It is difficult to say precisely at what point this becomes the better starting option, and if and when to move from one to the other, as experience is a vital factor as well as age. The teacher would be expected to show some discretion or experiment with different balls before concentrating on one, even having some pupils working with one type and others at a more advanced stage with another.

The ball size suggested for practices in this chapter is matched not to ages, but to children's needs at the point when a particular skill could first be attempted on a school playground.

Medium (or occasionally large) sized balls

1 Lifting, carrying and 'moving'
These practices will familiarise the children with the properties of the ball and begin the long process of learning to judge the forces required to control, propel and stop it.

a Pick the ball up off the floor with two hands and hold it in different positions: in front of the body, to the side, above the head and between the legs.

b Balance the ball on the flat palms of one or two hands and later attempt to move the ball into new positions – up/down, out/in and so on.

c 'Trap' the ball with the hand(s) against different parts of the body, ranging from the easy, eg tummy, to the more difficult, behind the back for example.

d Move about attempting **b** and **c**: sliding the feet, walking, jogging slowly, jumping and hopping.

e 'Roll' the ball along or over body parts with two hands and then one. Develop this by attempting to 'roll' it round one foot, keeping both ball and foot on the ground and then round the thigh, calf, neck and back.

2 'Steering' or hand dribbling
● Steer the ball anywhere in the playground. Keep it moving gently by following it and pushing it, or using a series of short finger taps. Use both hands or one only

● As in preceding activity but moving sideways or diagonally and, at a later stage, backwards

● Roll round both feet in a figure of eight. Later attempt to do it without touching the feet with the ball

- Steer or dribble round one marker, or in and out of a number of markers placed on the ground. The markers – domes, cones, beanbags or hoops – can be placed randomly or in lines and the spacing progressively reduced, eg from 3 or 4 metres to 1

- Steer to and stop on lines, or change direction on command

- Steer round circles, squares, along marked lines and so on

- Stop or change direction on teacher's command

- Steer the ball in and out of the other class members, with space restrictions making this more difficult

- Attempt many of the above practices with a specified hand or by changing hands on command.

This type of activity encourages observation, since pupils must not only watch the ball, but look around in order to avoid collisions by stopping, or through changes in speed and direction.

3 Rolling

Individual
- Roll the ball forwards slowly and follow. Pick it up when the ball slows down or stops

- Roll the ball out to the side, as above

- Roll forwards. Follow and stop it dead with hand(s) on top of the ball

- Roll forwards. Run round to face the ball and stop it with two flat hands, then one, then feet/foot

- Run round to face the ball and pick it up immediately

- Roll the ball. Run alongside and pick it up as it is moving

- Roll the ball in different directions. Either stop it and pick it up or pick it up as it moves

With partners
A rolls the ball to partner, **B**, over distances of 3 to 10 metres.

- Stop with two hands and then pick up

- Stop with one hand, two feet, one foot and so on

- Pick up immediately without stopping

- **B** adopts the half kneel side-on position used in fielding games, designed to stop the ball going through the legs

- Stop the ball by putting the foot on top of it

- **A** rolls the ball in a different direction (up to an angle of 90 degrees). **B** runs across and stops the ball using any method as described above. **B** returns the ball using a roll or, later, a throw or bounce

- As for preceding exercise but **B**, instead of returning the ball to a stationary **A**, rolls it in a new direction. The practice can then become continuous

- **A** rolls the ball gently past **B** who is standing with his/her back to **A**, facing the direction of roll. When the ball comes into sight **B** gives chase, picks it up and returns it as soon as possible initially by rolling but later, as skill improves, by throwing or bouncing. This practice simulates a real fielding game situation

- Rolling for accuracy – aiming to 'pass' between partners' feet (actually stopped by the hands). Distances between partners and feet can be adjusted to match individual and pairs' needs. *This activity can be scored – see Beanbags 15*

- Roll between two markers placed mid-way between the partners

- Rolling for speed – a specified number of times over a set distance, for example 5–25 metres depending on skill.

The rolling practices, most of which are worth attempting with a small ball at a later point, contribute to ball handling skill and also help in laying the foundations for the development of the more specific fielding skills that are employed in games such as rounders and cricket.

4 Bouncing

Individual
Throwing the ball up, initially just above the head then progressively higher.

a In front. Let it bounce until it stops or runs away

b Aim to catch after one or more bounces

c As for **a** and **b** but throw up at the side or over the head, turning round as quickly as possible

d As for **b** and **c** but throwing the ball higher

The practices described above put an excellent premium on accurate throwing, that is keeping the ball close to the body when throwing it up.

e Drop the ball from chest height and catch it after one bounce, if necessary, bending the knees

f 'Push' the ball down with two hands, to give greater force, and catch it; in front and to both sides of the body

g Using a hoop:

- bounce the ball in the hoop, which is placed in front or to the side, and catch it after each bounce

- stand in the hoop and bounce the ball outside on one spot – inside if it is large enough – and right round the outer edge

- stand in one hoop, bounce in another

- keep bouncing in a hoop while moving round the outer edge facing in

- walk on the hoop bouncing the ball round the outside or the inside

h Walk about throwing the ball up or 'forcing' it down, catching after one bounce. Vary the height of the throw or the force in the bounce to catch at different heights

i As for **h** but move in different directions

j Continuous bouncing. Aim to 'take' the ball down towards the ground with the hands, maintaining contact for as long as possible. Similarly aim to make contact as early as possible with the return bounce, moving the hands up with the ball. The arms move up and down with the ball, which should not be batted or 'hit' at the ground

k Continuous bouncing whilst moving: forwards and in different directions; round markers; in and out of spaced objects; along lines; in and out of fellow class members (first use two hands and then one; preferred, then non-preferred)

l Continuous bouncing with a hoop. Practices as for **g**

m As above but using the non-preferred hand or changing from one to the other

n Using two or one hand(s) put the ball through the legs or under one leg

o Practices using a target:

- bounce to hit a wall target, eg concentric circles or squares, or a hoop angled at the foot of the wall

- throw to a wall, not normally at a target, from increasing distances for the rebound to hit a ground target, eg the space between two parallel ropes, a skittle or a series of hoops

With partners

The following practices will help children to develop an understanding of how combining accurate direction with the correct distance and force will enable them to make a successful pass.

● Standing at gradually increasing distances (say 2 up to 7 metres) with one foot in front of the other, bounce the ball with two hands using a symmetrical arm action and catch it with both hands opposite the chest

● Bounce over a line – painted line, rope or cane

● Bounce the ball between two lines. The gap may be adjusted to cater for improvement through practice or increased throwing distance

● Bounce into hoops of different sizes at different distances

● Bounce through a hoop suspended or held vertically or slightly inclined, close to a wall. Alternatively work in threes – one holding, two bouncing

● Bounce – gently at first – in a different direction, initially no more than 20 degrees off 'line'. Partner runs to catch, stops and returns

● As above but continuously. **A** bounces for **B** to catch. **B** stops and then bounces in a new direction for **A** to catch, stop

● As above but the ball is bounced again as soon as it is received.

5 Throwing and catching
Many of the throwing and catching activities suggested for beanbags can also be done with a medium sized ball, the catch being made with two hands. Development in some cases would follow beanbag work; in others it could be done in parallel, depending in particular on the age of the participants.

Activities using the feet

Only basic, simple practices are covered in this unit. Further development would be undertaken as part of a specific football programme. In all the following practices it is assumed that the preferred foot is used first and that at a later point in time, the activities will be attempted with the non-preferred foot.

6 Passing and stopping the ball

Normally to a partner. Leave 3 metres between each pair and start 3 metres apart, increasing the distance between as competence improves.

● Push the ball using the inside edge of the foot, lifting the foot further back for increased distance. Partner stops the ball with the foot

● As above but using the toe; the top of the foot; the outside edge of the foot

● Push the ball between two beanbags adjusted for ability

● Kick along a marked line

● Pass for speed – return the ball without stopping it first

● Pass on the move in pairs down the length of the playground, moving down one side and returning up the other

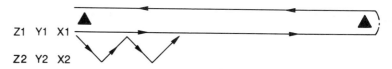

Z1 Y1 X1

Z2 Y2 X2

● Interpass down a column of skittles, each partner bringing the ball under control before making a pass back. Skittles should initially be widely spaced, eg 6 metres apart

X1

X2

X1 =
X2 =

● The ball is rolled at different speeds, while partners aim to stop it by using the side of the foot or putting the sole onto the ball.

7 Dribbling

Aim to keep the ball as close to the foot as possible while moving slowly. Improved control is shown by increased speed, and ability to change direction, using balls of different sizes. The children move in lines, or freely in space.

● Use inside edges of both feet, then right and left foot only

● Outside edges, toe and heel as above

● As above but stop the ball with sides or soles of feet on a signal. Continue dribbling on the next signal

● Protect the ball – game of 'Stealer':

A group of pupils with one ball each aim to prevent three other children from dispossessing them. Just one attempt to steal is allowed on another child, that is, one positive movement of the leg to 'reach' for the ball. No contact is allowed. If successful in collecting a ball it is retained; if not they move to another child. Dispossessed children are not allowed to attempt to retake from the classmate who took their own ball.

● Use dribbling circuits (*see Appendix 1*). The circuit can be timed and the children given opportunities to improve their personal records.

Activities using a stick

8 Pushing/hitting
A 'Unihoc' stick, plastic with a wide blade, is best but mini-hockey sticks or blades can also be used. Starting with the medium sized plastic or toughened sponge balls, progress is made by moving on to the 9cms sponge or airflow balls, which are still lighter and larger than a hockey ball.

Stand in pairs, 4 to 5 metres apart initially, although distance can be increased as control develops. Start by putting the stick behind the ball, touching the ground and pushing it forward, aiming to maintain contact with the ground and ball for as long as possible. As this is the simplest and most easily controlled method of passing the ball it would be wise to concentrate on it at first, covering a range of practices, before lifting the stick a little and hitting through the ball.

● Push the ball to a partner who stops it using the blade and pushes it back

● Development would be as for passing with the feet, as seen in Activity 6, eg hitting the ball between markers, along a line and passing on the move between pairs.

9 Dribbling
Walking, jogging slowly and finally running, aim to keep the ball as close to the blade as possible. Initially the blade can be put behind the ball and contact with the floor maintained throughout as the ball is steered around. Eventually a series of short, quick taps are used.

The development is similar to that used for dribbling with the feet in Activity 7, starting by moving in lines across a flat surface such as a playground or well cut grass pitch, and continuing by:

- moving in different directions
- round and in and out of markers
- in and out of class mates
- changing directions on signals
- using circuits (*see Appendix 1*)
- attempting a game of 'stealer'
- enjoying relays (*see Competition section and Appendix 2*).

Small balls

Balls of this size may be used for many of the practices outlined in the first section of this chapter, in most cases increasing the difficulty. They serve as a development for the catching practices listed for beanbags, especially those which can be attempted with one hand. They are also used in any activity where the ball is to be held tightly in one hand, thrown long distances or hit in the air by some sort of bat (see Unit 3).

The following practices are best attempted with a firm but yielding ball, which gives a good and consistent bounce, such as a tennis ball. Other balls of varying weight and bounce properties can be used later to increase difficulty and the range of experience.

1 Balancing
- On the palm and/or fingers (later on the back of the hand). Stand still and move the hand in different planes up/down, out/in, left/right and so on

- As for beanbag, for example changing shape and moving onto other body parts

- Moving across the floor in different ways: walking, running and sliding in different directions.

2 Bouncing

Individually
a Grip the ball and throw it hard at the ground

b Continuous one hand bouncing. Start by aiming to get the ball to bounce up to about waist height in front of the body, catching it each time and bouncing again immediately

c As above but the ball is 'patted' down each time with the palm of the slightly curved open hand (*See Medium balls Activity 4j*)

The following practices assume continuous bouncing, possibly catching the ball each time as in **b** but more probably patting as in **c**.

d Bounce wide out to the left and across to the far right in an arc and back again

e Keep the ball bouncing on a marked spot, eg the intersection of two painted lines. Move round it in a circle

f Hoop work as for medium balls

g Bounce to move the ball right round the body, transferring from one hand to the other behind the back

h Under each raised leg

i How quickly, that is, how many in a given time

j How softly or quietly; how close to the floor

k Keeping the feet on the ground, aim to bounce the ball round one or both legs

l Keep bouncing whilst changing body position: half kneel, kneel, sit, lie down on side and front, balance on seat and get up again

m Start by moving round one marker, then using two and three, gradually building up routes of increasing complexity (*see Appendix 1*)

i

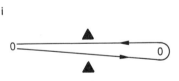

ii

iii

The following two practices are particularly valuable in that they enhance the ability to focus on both the movement of the ball, and the actions or movements of others at the same time.

n On command the pupils do what the teacher says. The teacher calls out a variety of ways of moving – drawn from those listed above – while bouncing the ball. He/she also commands the children to do things like watch another class member

o The pupils bounce while watching the teacher and aim to copy as soon as possible any of his/her actions. The teacher may, for example, put a hand on the head, stretch an arm out to the side, stand on one leg, crouch, move in different directions in different ways and change the dribbling hand. *Although the teacher may simulate the action of bouncing, a ball is not actually used.*

With partners
a Bounce for one handed catching from a distance of 4 to 7 metres. Both right and left hands are used to catch.

b As for **a** but move to the ball forwards and sideways

c Bounce into a hoop. *Beat the record* or other competitions can take place either bouncing in free space or into a hoop

For distance

d Hold the arm up above the shoulder and whip the ball forwards, pushing forward from the shoulder and flicking the wrist. Aim for distances of up to 10 metres

e Use a full overarm throw (*see Activity 4*) in order to increase the distance the ball travels before bouncing

f Aim for lines – either marked or using ropes – and hoops to increase accuracy and distance and also to aid partners' positioning in relation to the bounce.

3 Rolling
a For distance – can increase considerably on what can be achieved with the medium sized balls

b For speed – aiming to pick up the ball and return it in one action. The pick-up can be done with two hands initially and then attempted with one. The ball can be returned with a roll, a bounce or a throw to hand

c As for the 'fielding game' described in *Medium balls* rolling section. The speeds and distances involved tend to be greater

d For simulating game conditions. One partner, **A**, takes up a recognized receiving position, eg foot on a rounders base, in a hoop or behind a set of stumps, or two skittles placed together to simulate wickets. **A** rolls or throws out a ball to different distances and in different direction. **B** fields and aims to return the ball so accurately with a roll that **A** does not have to move. Distances start short and increase with capability.

e Very similar to **d** but working in threes.

A and **B** are as before but this time **C** is stationed 5–10 metres in front of **A**. As before **A** rolls or throws out, with distances tending towards the maximum as used in **d** and beyond. **B** returns as quickly as possible by rolling the ball towards **A**. **C** moves immediately to the actual pathway of the ball and picks it up, moving it on to **A** with an accurate roll, or later, a throw.

4 Throwing and catching

Short – underarm
a In pairs. **A** places the ball beside the foot on the preferred hand side and then bends down, possibly on the teacher's signal, and picks it up. **A** throws in one action to **B** who is standing about 4 metres away, aiming for the stomach.

b As for **a** but the ball is placed 2 to 3 metres in front of **A** who, on the signal, has to run forward, pick up the ball and throw to **B**.

c As for **b** but the approach is a fast sideways shuffle, so that when the ball is picked up the body is already in the best position for throwing longer distances, with weight on the back foot as in a distance throw. **B** stands at greater distances from the ball.

Long – overarm
The long term intention is to develop a good throwing action – standing slightly sideways on, with weight on the back foot and the back leg slightly bent, lean backwards a little and stretch out the throwing arm. Throw hard by bending the arm at the elbow and 'pulling' the ball over the top of the shoulder, while at the same time transferring the weight onto the front foot and straightening the body. Follow through for maximum distance; the back foot may be dragged past the front. Aim to match pairs by ability.

- Throw hand to hand aiming to increase distance. The height of the arc of the throw should increase with distance, the angle of release moving up to a maximum of 45 degrees

- Throw for partners to run forwards or sideways in order to catch the ball directly or after a bounce.

Using a target
- Work in pairs to hit a small target placed in the centre of circles (size matched to ability): a skittle, quoit or beanbag

- Throw to hit a wall target – normally concentric rings:

i Ten throws of a designated type at a specified distance. Keep score and repeat, aiming to improve.

ii With each successful hit on a particular ring move one step further away. Compete against a partner.

iii Rapid fire throwing and catching with two or one hand(s), possibly timed, eg how many catches in the span of 15 seconds.

Wall target working with a partner
- Stand side by side, throwing and catching alternately. The throwing, catching and distance can all be varied

- Keep the ball moving in a straight line, partners interchanging

- Offset throwing. The children stand at different distances and angles from the target.

As there are not sufficient wall targets in the majority of schools for the whole class to all work on at once, the activities described above would probably have to be incorporated in a groupwork system (see Unit 7).

5 'Patting'
Bouncing the balls off the palm of the hands upwards into the air.

- Aim to increase the number of pats on each hand. Encourage the pupils to keep the bounce fairly low.

- Transfer from one hand to the other, and back again.

- Attempt many of the ideas as listed under Carrying (*Medium Balls no. 1*) or Bouncing (*Medium no. 4 and no. 2 above*), particularly those involving changes in body position and height, and moving round or in and out of obstacles and classmates.

6 Bowling

Cricket type

All middle to top juniors can attempt this skill working in pairs.

- Aim to bowl in a straight line to a partner. Start by standing sideways on to the direction of bowling. The bowling arm is outstretched in line with the shoulder and is kept straight throughout the action. Both the outstretched non-bowling arm and the front foot are pointed towards the partner. As the shoulders are swung round to face the front and the weight moved on to the front foot, the bowling arm is swung over the shoulder very close to the head, and the ball released with a slight downward action of the wrist

- Aim for lines (chalked or ropes) or a large hoop about 15 metres from the release point

- Cricket stumps (either spring-back or painted on a wall) can be aimed for after the bounce in groupwork.

Rounders type
- **A** stands with the front foot in one hoop and bowls so that the ball (at stomach height) should pass over another, smaller, hoop positioned in front of the receiver **B**, thus encouraging accuracy in line

- Working in threes, bowl through a hoop held at around stomach height.

7 Activities using the feet
Many of the passing and dribbling activities suggested for medium balls can be attempted, but the skill involved is much greater.

Additionally

- Use the sole of the foot to control the ball; stopping it, 'hiding' it or pulling it sideways, particularly before moving in a new direction

- Shield the ball. Partner **A** stands with the ball just in front of his/her feet. Partner **B** stands one metre behind **A**. On the signal **B** aims to get round **A** and to dispossess him/her. **A** aims to keep possession by keeping the body between the ball and **B**. The ball is touched or moved occasionally but the object is to guard it rather than to dribble vast distances. Time limits can be used, starting as low as five seconds and moving to 10, 15 and so on.

Competitions

Medium/large or small balls may both be used and in some cases, particularly the passing activities, rugby balls provide both a skilful and fun alternative.

1 Non-relay
Activities suggested for beanbags may also be attempted with balls although, because of the space required to house the balls, it may be better only to attempt 'Keep the kettle boiling' with the smaller variety.

2 Relays

a As for beanbags

b 'Spry' type – see Appendix 2

c In threes – straight line
A and **B** stand with legs apart. The ball is rolled back by **A** through **B**'s legs and is only touched by **B** if it goes off line. **C** on receiving the ball turns round to face the opposite way (as do **A** and **B**) and rolls it back, the process being repeated any number of times without anyone having to move from the spot. Later **C** may run to the front and roll the ball back and so on.

With rugby balls it would be advisable to allow all pupils to help steer the ball through and to keep the gaps between pupils to a minimum.

d In threes or fours – using a bench
i The children stand astride the bench and roll the ball along it. Positions can be reversed, or the back pupil may run to the front to continue.

ii The children stand on the bench and pass the ball back through the legs. Children enjoy this activity very much since with a medium and, particularly, a large sized ball they have to adopt well emphasised bow leg positions.

iii The ball is passed back over the heads or alternately, over and through.

e Semi–shuttle

A starts with the ball and rolls, bounces, throws or kicks it to **B**. It must cross line 2. Both **A** and **B** run forward, with **B** turning on crossing line 1. **B** rolls, bounces, throws or kicks the ball to **C** with **A** taking up a position directly behind **C**. The process thus becomes continuous with the ball always projected in the same direction. To ensure that there is no coming forward to meet the ball a skittle may be placed on each of the two lines, with the ball received on one side and the run forward made from the other.

line 1   line 2

————— = rolling ball

· · · · · · · · = running path

f In pairs – basic relay system (see Appendix 2)

i The ball is steered on the floor round two markers

ii The ball may be bounced and caught, 'patted' up by the hand or dribbled by hand. In each case the ball is always handed to the partner, never thrown, bounced or rolled.

iii The ball is dribbled round using foot, feet or stick. Transfer can be by allowing a short pass after the player has rounded the back marker, or by stopping the ball on a designated spot, for example a chalked circle or hoop.

Flat bats

These will be of various dimensions and shapes, basically round or rectangular.

Choice will depend on the skill and strength of the individual and the activity to be undertaken. In general it would be wise to avoid the very small versions, while the larger, rectangular type are best for the more advanced games.

The bats can be used with shuttlecocks and a variety of balls: sponge, soft rubber, tennis, and airflow. Airflow, because they do not bounce as fast or as far as others, can be particularly useful.

1 Balancing
- The ball is balanced on the bat held in front of the body

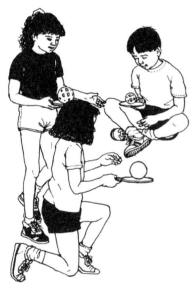

- The bat can be moved in different planes, for example up and down, and at different speeds

- The body can be moved – to crouch, sit, lie and so on

- A range of movements across the floor can be done: walking, jogging and jumping in different directions, or manœuvring round and through markers and fellow class members.

Additionally the above can be attempted by turning the wrist over and using the other surface of the bat (backhand), or with the non-preferred hand.

2 Hitting – individually
The following practices will help to develop bat/eye/ball coordination but not in a specific game stroke playing sense.

a Hit the ball up, let it bounce, hit up and so on. With increasing control the ball can be hit higher or the hit can be directed so that the ball lands on a spot or drops in a hoop

b Keep the ball up through continuous hitting, starting out close to the bat

c As for **b** but moving as in balancing activities

d As for **c** but using backhand or changing from forehand to backhand

e Bat the ball down hard onto the floor. Allow two or more bounces until the ball is at an appropriate height and hit it again

f Hit continuously to the floor, while stationary or moving in ways described above

g Hit to a wall:

- with or without a bounce

- extending distance with practice.

3 Hitting – partners

All types of balls can be tried but, since balls like tennis balls tend to 'fly', airflow and sponge can make it easier for more children to achieve initial success.

a Hit gently 'to and fro' with one bounce in between. With success, using ten successive bounces as a criterion, move on to try backhands and both hands

b As for **b** but volleying

c Use a painted line or skipping rope. Aim to hit the ball so that it bounces on the opposite side of the rope each time that it is struck

d As above but competing, against all other pairs, or using *Beat the Record*

e As for **d** but volleying or using backhands

f Volley over a high barrier: a net, rope or cane attached to posts set at a height of about 1½ metres plus

g Hit alternately to a reasonably smooth wall – with a bounce or volley, forehand, backhand or a mixture of both. Play:

- side by side

- stepping in and out to maintain a straight line flight

- hitting at angles

- as above but changing speed, height of contact on the wall and distance

h Partner **A** stands near and with their back to a wall. The other partner, **B**, throws the ball underarm and at moderate speed, within stretch reach of **A**. **B** aims at the wall which **A** defends with the bat

i **A** bowls underarm as in a game like rounders. **B** hits the ball back for catches.

*This may be seen as the first step in learning to hit a ball forward as in a striking game. However it should not be practised for too long as it tends to teach hitting **to** rather than **away from** other players.*

4 Hitting – in fours
Use small courts, say 6 × 3 metres, marked by playground lines, chalk, or even ropes or beanbags at each corner. Hit over a low net, cane(s) placed on skittles or posts, or a bench. Play with two a side.

a Cooperation – all players assist each other in keeping the ball going
● with a bounce at each side

● no bounce

● mixture of bounce and volleys either in order or randomly

b Playing a competition – scoring points
Older pupils may be invited to decide their own systems for bringing the ball into play, and scoring and rules (*see Appendix 3*). The best systems are those which

● score a point for each rally, unlike say badminton or squash

● allow successive serving to a numerical limit like table-tennis before the ball goes to the other side and

● keep the winning score low, eg 11 points with a margin of two clear points, allowing for early adjustment of pairs or opponents.

c Further advancement of batting and bowling practice

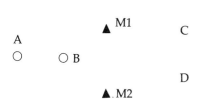

B, with front foot in a hoop as marked or behind a line, bowls to **A** aiming for the ball to pass over a small hoop placed to the side of **A**, and between knee and shoulder. **A** must hit the ball forward so that it passes between the two markers **M1** and **M2** and aiming to avoid the two fielders, **C** and **D**. If there is any likelihood of the ball being missed by the batter, then one of the two fielders can act as a backstop.

Interest can be sustained or increased by introducing simple scoring. **A** receives say, six, eight or ten balls and, starting with ten points, scores an additional two for every ball that passes between the markers and beats **B**, **C** and **D**. **B**, **C** and **D** score three points for every catch taken and one point for every ball taken first bounce.

This practice encourages hitting the ball hard along the ground or aiming for space. All pupils have an opportunity to practice bowling and there is an incentive to field well. It is even possible to award points to fielders for returning the ball accurately to the bowler, say if his/her foot remains in the hoop.

5 With shuttlecocks
a All the volleying practices listed previously for individual, pairs and fours work with balls using a high net or rope attached to securely anchored posts.

b As for **4b** above – develop a game using a court, paying particular attention to the dimensions which will produce the best result. This could lead to playing a version of the adult game of batinton, a game based on the badminton court, net and rules.

Short handled racquets

These are specially designed tennis racquets with lightweight frames and short handles, which make it much easier for young children to play rallies, particularly with sponge type balls.

Basic practices are the same as for flat bats.

Further development leads to the game of short tennis, requiring a net of the correct size, marked courts and so forth.

Rounders bats

Basic hitting practices, as outlined for flat bats, can be under-taken by older children using this equipment – the mini cricket bat shape (approximately 7.5cm broad) is much easier for junior children to handle than the thin rounders sticks. Similarly, a ball such as a tennis or an airflow ball will help the children to achieve greater success and develop more confidence than if they were to use the smaller, harder rounders ball.

1 'Passing'

Moving the quoit without it travelling through the air. The activities are basically the same as for the beanbag, for example round the back, over the head or shoulders and through the legs, each time passing from hand to hand.

- Variations: in balance positions

- The quoit is 'hooked' onto the foot and transferred either to the other foot while sitting or to a partner's foot while standing.

2 Throwing and catching

The following practices add variety to the catching range. Good judgement of pace, trajectory and the position of the quoit is essential before the object can be grasped.

Individually

a Throw the quoit up using one hand. Catch with two hands, then with right, left. Start about one metre above the head and increase height as competence develops

b Throw the quoit up so that it comes down flat (horizontal). Aim to catch it as above

c As for **b** but

i aim to thrust the hand through

ii aim to thrust a unihoc stick through

d Throw the quoit up so that it wobbles or spins in flight and aim to catch as before, first with two, then separate hands

e Many practices for beanbags may be used, eg touching different body parts, clapping, catching opposite different body parts or jumping to catch.

With partners

Start 3 metres apart and increase distance with success.

a Throw vertically and horizontally and catch with two hands, then one

b Throw with a variety of angles, wobbles and spins

c The range of activities as listed for beanbags

d One partner holds a hockey or unihoc stick with the handle projecting at about 45 degrees. The other aims to throw the quoit so that it drops over the end of the stick and slides down the shaft. The stick may or may not be moved by the holder in order to assist the thrower. Alternatively one partner throws the quoit up high so that the other can attempt to thrust the stick through it

e As for the first activity in **d**, but with the stick held the other way round. The partner aims to hook the quoit over the blade

3 Rolling

The quoit will not roll unless it is released in the correct way. The action is akin to that used in the game of bowls, with the palm of the hand half under and half behind the vertically held quoit, fingers pointing in the direction of the roll. The quoit is released as close to the ground as possible with the fingers giving the spin that ensures that it rolls, not skids, along the ground. Working with a partner at a starting distance of about 4 metres:

a Roll for partner to stop the quoit using feet, foot, hands and hand

b Partner aims to pick the quoit up without stopping it first. First use two hands, then one hand (the preferred hand first followed by the non-preferred)

c Aim to improve the line of the roll by rolling between the partner's feet; between two beanbags or markers; to hit a cone or skittle with the partner standing behind; along a line

d Roll for distance, aiming to cross a series of lines

e Aim to control the length of the roll combining accuracy with distance. Roll so that the quoit stops

● between two lines

● near to or in a circle or hoop

f Attempt to roll past a partner who defends a section of a line marked with cones or beanbags

g Aim to pick the quoit up as it rolls past or is chased, using one hand or the blade of a unihoc or hockey stick.

4 'Flicking'

Activities such as these, although not related to known game skills, are valuable in extending the range of practices in which thought must be given to the force and action of the leg movement to produce the desired effect.

The quoit is balanced on top of, or hooked on to, one foot. Activities as for the beanbag (*Unit 1, Activity 14*):

- to clear an obstacle or bar

- to hit a target on a wall or on the ground.

5 Floor object

The quoit can be used, like the beanbag, as an object placed on the floor to move over in a variety of ways, for balance work or to touch.

6 Competitions

a In relays the quoit may be passed from hand to hand as an alternative to batons, beanbags or touching, for example in a race round markers

b In relays use the quoit as a substitute for a ball or beanbag where the object is

- rolled or slid

- passed from hand to hand in a team through legs and over heads, and when standing on or astride a bench

- thrown

c 'Deck tennis'

Use a small court adjusted to match ability, with a net around badminton height (1½ metres). Two play against two.

Each player serves five, as in table tennis, with teams alternating and each rally being scored. Apart from service, which is taken from behind the back line, the quoit is thrown over the net from where it is received, with the feet remaining on the floor. There should be no lets; the quoit must completely clear the net each time. Points are won if *i* the quoit is dropped by an opponent, *ii* the opponents throw it out of court and *iii* when a one hand rule is applied, if the quoit is caught with two. In advanced versions the quoit may be allowed to wobble or spin in the air, but not on service.

This game could be an alternative to Activity 1 in Groupwork Example 3 (*Unit 7*).

The first set of these activities (1–4) are of a basic movement or gymnastic type. They can be attempted as part of a whole class or groupwork orientated small apparatus programme, or integrated into gymnastic lessons to encourage more variety and precision in a range of movements and balances.

Skipping ropes

Ideally these will be individual, of short to medium length.

1 Moving over or along a rope laid in a straight line on the ground
a Walk, jump or hop along the rope forwards, backwards and sideways. Crawl along the rope using hands and feet, or hands and knees; semi-crawl using two hands and one foot, one hand and two feet and so on. Difficult movements requiring very good control, such as cartwheels and walking on the hands, can also be attempted by talented gymnasts.

b Move over the rope from one side to the other either continuously or preferably, stopping still after each movement.

c Jump or hop in a variety of ways; 'tip' over the rope to finish and ultimately balance on different body parts or combinations of body parts, eg seat, tummy, hands and one knee. Try hand and feet movements including the relatively simple, where contact for both with the floor is maintained virtually all the time, eg crawling, and the progressively more difficult, which involve lifting the seat and/or feet to greater heights, eg a bunny jump or cartwheel. Educational gymnastics limitation tasks can be used to great advantage in this activity, specifying degrees of stretch and direction.

2 Moving round a rope made into a shape on the ground
The shapes may be open or closed and are normally based on mathematical figures or letters. Teachers can dictate a shape to be used by the whole class or children may choose their own. Straight line forms such as squares, triangles and the letter V can be balanced against curvy forms such as circles, ovals and letters such as C, S, and U.

43

a Move along the rope as in **1a**

b Use a particular movement to go right round the outside of the shape, eg a square, or, if a letter, to follow its contours. Examples could be hopping or two hands and two feet used symmetrically.

c Move round using a repeated pattern of different movements, for example a bunny jump, a jump and a roll or three different jumps

d Follow the shape while at the same time crossing the rope.

3 Moving over two ropes
The ropes may be placed in parallel lines or angled from a common point.

a The area between the ropes is taboo: pretend that it is a river. The object is to get from one side of the ropes to the other using a variety of movements, with and without a short run-up. In the case of the angled ropes (normally with about 30 degrees between them) there is the additional objective of getting as far down the ropes as possible, thus increasing the distance with each attempt.

b The area in between may be touched by one part of the body only, eg foot/feet, hands/hand. Movements begin as simple as a hop or two-foot sideways jump, and progress to normal and one-arm cartwheels. It is an ideal way to encourage children to attempt to walk on their hands, that is to take two 'steps' to get across.

4 Shapes and balances using one or two ropes
a A single rope or two in parallel can again represent taboo territory. The children make bridges over the rope(s) using different parts of the body and aiming for varied shapes.

b The children hold set shapes or balances while maintaining contact with one or two ropes. Different numbers of contact points may be employed and the children can be encouraged to use, or be limited to, specified parts of the body.

5 Skipping – on the spot
a The easiest mode of skipping for most young children is a galloping or running action on the spot. The best way to teach the activity is as follows:

● Allow the children to attempt the action, checking that the rope is being rotated at the correct length. If reasonably successful continue to practice, preferably little and often at first, until the action is both confident and consistent.

- If not successful hold the rope in the correct starting position behind the calves or heels and rotate it over the head, onto the floor in front of the toes. As soon as it is still take a walking step over it. Repeat a few times until competent.

- Speed up the process so that 'running' over it rapidly is encouraged.

- Aim to move the rope back on the floor as soon as it lands.

- Stress that the actions should be joined together so that there are no stops and starts. If this is done successfully the pupils will be virtually skipping – simply encourage them to move a little bit quicker so that the arms circle at a constant speed.

b Double-foot jump action, with a little bounce before the rope passes under the feet: 'basic' skipping. The action can be attempted and taught in the same way as **a**, with the substitution of a jump for the walking step. When this is mastered many variations are possible:

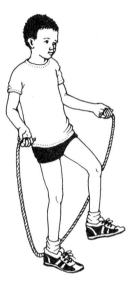

- skipping by moving the rope backwards and sideways

- changing body shape – wide down to tucked, remembering to shorten the rope as the body contracts

- odd shapes, eg one arm high, one low

- turning round on the spot

- with straight legs – kicked out to the front alternately

- on one foot, the heels and so on

- crossed arms, crossed legs, dance type steps

- pupils invent their own

- combinations of the above, eg hopping with rope moved sideways

c 'Pepper' skipping
No small bounce, just one floor contact per revolution

6 Skipping – moving across the hall floor or playground
- Move forwards using many of the actions/modes outlined above, with variations based on both the running and the double foot methods

- Move sideways and, carefully, backwards with the rope moving forwards, backwards or sideways, possibly varying leg action as above

7 Skipping – sequences

The skipper starts with one mode, moves to another without stopping and without showing any perceptible break then moves to a third and so on. Three or four modes could be accepted as a basic sequence, with six being a reasonable target for most top juniors providing they have been allowed sufficient practice to master a range of separate skipping techniques before attempting to join them. Sequences can be done on the spot, moving across the floor or can combine elements of both.

8 Skipping with a partner – using one rope

● side by side – some variations are possible

● in line, either face to face or facing the same way, one turning the rope. Normally both skip in exactly the same way

● one partner moves in and out.

9 Skipping with a partner – using two ropes

a Follow my Leader or 'Copy cat'. A starts to skip in a given way. **B** must copy on the spot or follow across the playground.

b Synchronised skipping. Both partners aim for a perfect shadow image with respect to mode and timing. Partners may stand side by side, facing each other in a 'mirror' image or stand one behind the other.

c Synchronised skipping sequences. These may be considered the ultimate in skipping control. Combining 7 and 9 **b** the partners aim to work together in producing a varied, continuous and perfectly matched sequence. As with the solo sequences it is best to concentrate on, say, just three modes until they are perfectly joined, that is, with no perceptible break. Add further modes one at a time, with six being a good target to aim for (*see 4. Free Choice, Unit 7*).

10 Skipping to music

Most of the activities outlined above may be set to musical accompaniment. This will add interest and bring in a new dimension, timing.

11 Skipping in groups

A lot of enjoyment can be gained from larger numbers (of three children up to the whole class if proficient) attempting to synchronise one or more types of skipping. Alternatively, have some children working on matched modes and others on contrasting forms. Music can be very helpful if large numbers are involved.

Not only do all the skipping modes described above give excellent opportunities for developing specific movement control but frequent inclusion of skipping work can also help to counter the claim that the heart rate is not raised often enough or high enough in physical education lessons.

12 Additional activities

a Double the rope and hold at each end. Pass round the body – over the head, down the back and under one foot at a time. Bring the hands in closer or double the rope again and pass round as before.

b Double the rope and hold each end. Hold in position in front of the feet as if to skip and raise a few inches off the floor. The children attempt to jump over it, normally with two feet together.

13 Competitions

• First to jump, hop or use two hands to cross the rope, laid in a straight line on the ground, a set number of times

• Skipping – on the spot and across the floor or round an obstacle, returning to the starting position. Can also be done as a small team relay (twos or threes).

Long rope

Group skipping
Two children turn the rope, varying length and speed. Two or more children skip, possibly using the same mode, shadowing, moving in and out, or holding hands and so on.

Safety
*Ropes of any description should **not** be used as 'bars', attached to high jump stands or skittles for jumping activities. A bar manufactured for this purpose, a cane or a piece of coloured elastic will not only be much safer, but will present a more consistent target to clear. (see* Unit 8 Safety*)*

Hoops

The hoops may be of different sizes. In some activities the size will make little difference (eg jumping in when laid on the floor); in others, the smaller the hoop the more difficult the execution of the activity, for example moving in or through without touching, when raised from the floor. Moving from medium sized or sometimes large hoops to smaller sizes can be seen as part of a progression.

Most of the activities described (1–8) can be seen as excellent additions to the gymnastics programme. Interesting and very challenging work is possible, not only as a whole class activity, which has the advantage of being set up very easily and requiring minimum space, but in gymnastic groupwork (see Unit 7).

For the first set of activities the hoops are spaced evenly about the floor or playground with a gap of 1–4 metres between them, depending on activity, age and space available.

1 Moving between hoops
Demands accuracy and a keen awareness of the movement of others.

● Walk or run in the spaces without touching the hoops. Speed and mode of walking may be changed.

● Use other prescribed ways or limitation tasks, for example moving sideways, on hands and feet or in a given shape.

2 Moving inside a hoop
● Change shape inside the hoop without touching the sides, eg high, wide or small.

● Move onto different body parts, again with the eventual aim of not touching the hoop.

● As above but combine this with holding static finishing positions.

3 'Tipping' or 'Dropping' into a hoop

Starting from a stationary position outside the hoop, move onto a different part of the body, eg from two feet dropping backwards to finish on the seat, the hands remaining off the floor throughout.

4 Jumping activities

The following activities are excellent for extending the range of jumping and landing tasks, demanding varying degrees of power as well as control and initiative. Used often they can also help counter the claim that physical education makes insufficient demands on pupils in terms of 'exercise'.

a with the hoop(s) on the ground

i Stand close to and facing the hoop, two feet together. Jump in and after a pause, jump out again. The whole range of ideas as described for the beanbag can be used, with the added incentive of aiming for the dead centre of the hoop as the children become capable of such precision.

ii Two phase movements – jumping in and out again immediately. Changes of direction and different forms of jumping can be used.

iii With a run. From a short distance or using a specified number of steps (three or five at most), take off at first from two feet, to establish good control, and later from one.

iv A series of two or more hoops can be used in a line (straight or curved) or shape (triangle, square, circle, rectangle) with the gap between them extending to, for example, half a metre according to age and ability. The pupils jump from hoop to hoop using a particular 'line' or invented pattern. Stop and move or continuous modes can be used and other variations of height and direction employed.

b With the hoop held horizontally

The hoop – of medium size initially, since the large sizes are too big to be held firmly – is held in a full or half kneeling position as illustrated. Pupils attempting to jump in (or using any other movement) always approach from the side, never head on. Providing the hoop is held by just one child the activities are perfectly safe, the hoop simply swinging away when touched. The hoop must never be held by two children or pupils catching the hoop will fall.

i The hoop is held at a constant and comfortable height, from 15–40cms, depending on ability. The pupils may jump in a wide variety of ways: with and without a run, one/two foot take-off, into/out of, in different directions, with and without touching the rim.

ii The hoop is raised gradually, the children aiming to beat their own records. Pupils holding the hoops can be given a more positive role by being asked to help in assessing their partner's capabilities and setting challenging but attainable targets.

c **With the hoop held vertically or at an angle**
Starting with a large hoop held upright on the floor the pupils jump through, attempting different angles of approach and directions of movement. The hoop can be raised to different heights and a run-up added.

The hoop can then be held at different angles both on the floor and in the air, with inclination away from the jumper being much easier than towards. The large hoop can still be used for positions on the floor but a medium size is easier to handle when held above the ground.

5 Movements off or onto the hands
a With the hoop on the floor possibly in conjunction with a mat.

i From a crouch position the hands may be placed in, or more usually alongside, the hoop. The feet are lifted into the air and placed in the hoop in a bunny jump movement, a sideways approach being the easiest to start with. The movement can also be done forwards, backwards and with a twist, in each case starting off on one foot and keeping the other in the air. The pupils may also be encouraged to lift their seats high, get their feet higher than their bottoms and finally see how close to the sky or ceiling they can get one or both feet, before finishing in the hoop.

ii Using a cartwheel. This can be an interesting challenge to those pupils able to attempt cartwheels as the 'line' of approach and the distance must be exactly right in order to get the feet inside the hoop.

b With the hoop held horizontally as described in **4b** – initially very low – the children attempt to use the hands to get in with or without touching. Approaches can be made from different angles and good lift is needed to clear the hoop, particularly when raised.

c With the hoop held on or off the floor, vertical or slightly inclined, the body is tucked up and moved through, either off the hands or by putting them through and on to the floor, with a mat on the other side.

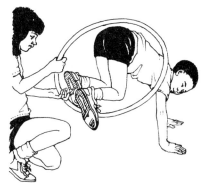

Crawling movements could be acceptable as a simple way of negotiating the hoops held in this way.

6 Rolling activities
● With the hoop flat on the floor *i* crouch inside and roll out: forwards, sideways or backwards – body tucked – normally on to a mat and *ii* from outside the hoop, moving into it, 'half' roll forwards to finish balanced on the seat, or seat and feet together, or as a half measure, the back. A 'half' roll sideways or backwards can finish on the shoulders, back or knees, ideally inside the hoop without touching the edge.

● With the hoop held vertically or angled slightly towards the performer, roll through from a crouch position. All directions are possible when the hoop is touching or close to the floor.

● As above but raising the hoop gradually – forward roll only, on to a mat.

7 Sliding activities
The hoop is held horizontally, starting at around 40cms above the ground, and is progressively lowered to increase difficulty. Sliding or slithering activities are best done on smooth hall floors.

● on the front initially, and also the back or the side, slide forwards or backwards right under the hoop from one side to the other

● slide on the front, back or side, moving forwards or backwards to come up through the hoop, aiming not to touch it. Step out

● step into the hoop and slide out from underneath

● limit floor contact with specified body parts, eg seat or tummy with hands; shoulders and feet.

Pupils may be allowed to experiment and those holding the hoop encouraged to make adjustments in height, particularly in the early stages, to enable successful negotiation to be made.

The activities described above are an extension of gymnastic apparatus work where, unlike the normal fixed and portable apparatus, the height and angles can be adjusted precisely to suit individual needs.

8 Balance activities

a Hoop on the floor

i Hold balances still inside the hoop, possibly after moving into it in a given way (see static finishing positions, Activities 1 and 2), eg on seat, shoulders, hip, two hands/one foot and so on

ii Balance across the hoop with either one or more parts inside and one or more parts outside the hoop or, using a small hoop, all parts on the outside, eg hands and feet to make a wide bridge

iii Keep one or more parts in contact with the hoop, for example hands on the hoop (no part to touch the floor) and one knee inside; shoulders inside and two feet on the hoop.

iv Balance entirely on the hoop using two feet; one foot; two hands and one foot.

v As for iv but work in pairs. Balances range from the relatively easy, with both standing on two feet, to one supporting the other in a handstand position, again with the aim of no contact with the floor.

vi As for iv and v but moving round the hoop.

b Counterbalance

Work in groups, starting and concentrating on pairs but also using threes and fours.

i Two or more pupils are inside the hoop. Starting with both feet together on the floor, the hoop is positioned against a variety of body parts and the pupils lean outwards. The back at waist height is the easiest position to start with. Others are tummies, necks, sides, backs of knees and so on

ii As for i but move either in a circular pattern across the floor or by rotating within the hoop, or both

iii The hoop is 'wedged' between two parts of the body, possibly the same but not necessarily so, in a vertical or horizontal plane, eg back to back, tummy to tummy or tummy to back

iv As in iii but moving across the floor

v The children stand on the outside of the hoop and grip it with two hands, although one hand can be used as a more advanced practice. They then lean outwards adopting either a sitting or, preferably, a straight body position. Variation and greater difficulty can be achieved by, for example, standing on one leg, adopting kneeling or sitting positions or using the 'crook' of the elbow.

c Balancing the hoop

Normally working with a group of three children although some of the balances are possible with two.

i The hoop is balanced on a variety of body parts, not held. Use hands, heads, arms, fingertips, shoulders (side of the neck), upper back, chest, nose, thighs, knees (while sitting, lying or crouching), one foot and the soles of one foot or both while lying on the back.

ii Some of the above can be attempted while moving, either round in a circle or across the floor.

d With a balance bar

The hoop is used to add variety to or increase the difficulty of dynamic balance activities carried out on primary gymnastic balance bars, bench ribs (ie bench turned upside down) or, for many infants and some juniors with poor control, the bench top itself.

i The hoop is held parallel to the balance bar, starting with a small gap between the two, say 10cms. Pupils walk along the bar and step into and out of the hoop, continuing along the bar to the end. Pupils with good control can be challenged further by using different directions; limiting the parts of the feet that may be used; turning round in the hoop and moving back to the original starting position; raising the level of the hoop above the bar and attempting any of the activities already described.

ii Stand inside hoop and aim to touch the bar outside the rim with different parts of the body.

iii Again start by standing inside the hoop, aiming to take up new balance positions with weight on different parts of the body. Parts may or may not be allowed on the floor beside the rib according to ability. The object is not to touch the hoop, either during the movement or in the final balance position.

iv The hoop is held vertically or at slightly inclined angles, touching the bar. Pupils aim to get through, ultimately without touching.

v As above, with the hoop raised to different heights above the rib. Angles as far down as 45 degrees may be used.

vi The hoop is held by the child who is balancing and rotated slowly round the body with skipping action. The child can remain on the spot or walk along the rib. The action can be reversed so that it is done backwards, and backward or sideways walking attempted.

vii The hoop is again held in positions parallel to the bar, with the objective this time being to move underneath it without touching. Walking – leaning forward or crouched – different forms of crawling and sliding can all be attempted.

Use of apparatus such as the hoop and the beanbag in this way undoubtedly adds real purpose to the work. Pupils sustain their interest for longer, enjoy repeating and extending over periods of time and, coming back to the activities after intervals of rest, show more rapid improvement in attaining higher levels of control and in trying alternative ways of answering a task. As with other activities this work can be done with the whole class, if there are sufficient benches and balance bars, or as part of groupwork. Tasks may be specific or of the limitation type, eg all movements must be sideways, use hands and feet and so forth.

9 Moving the hoop – round the body

• hold the hoop on the ground vertically or place horizontally in front of the feet. Step through and pull over the head to return the hoop to the original position

• skip with the hoop, forwards or backwards, on the spot or across the hall/playground. Many of the modes suggested for ropes can be attempted

• spin the hoop on different parts of the body: arm, wrist, finger, neck, waist and leg.

10 Moving the hoop – along the ground

a Rolling
Technique – hold the hoop still with the palm of the non-preferred hand on the top. Place the palm of the preferred hand with fingers pointing towards the ground at the back of the hoop and pull up and over maintaining contact for as long as possible to set it rolling.

i Between partners for accuracy or speed, starting at, say, 4 metres and gradually increasing the distance.

ii Using a small – medium sized hoop, rolled between partners. A third child aims to jump the hoop facing head-on and splitting the legs. Can also be attempted from the side, using a two-foot tucked jump or a 'scissors' technique.

iii Imparting reverse spin. The hoop is throw through the air and at the same time is set revolving backwards. It will return to the sender on contacting the ground.

b Bowling

Move alongside the hoop, using the palm and side of the hand to keep it rolling. Work only in large areas, eg a good sized playground, and on fairly flat surfaces. A number of variations are possible: using preferred or non-preferred hands: walking; jogging; running; freely; straight; along marked lines; around or through markers; changing directions or hands.

Pupils are encouraged to develop good 'vision' while doing this activity, since they will have to be looking around as well as controlling the hoop.

11 Moving the hoop – through the air

• Throw to partner over short distances

• As above but a second pair aim to throw a beanbag or ball through the hoop as it moves through the air.

12 Fun activities and competitions

a 'Chariots'. This game is played in pairs. One, the horse, stands inside the hoop and grips it at waist height while the other, the driver, stands outside the hoop facing the same direction as the horse and again gripping it at waist height. Pairs run in and out of each other with drivers steering by using a slight left or right depression of the hoop. This activity is hugely popular with infants and lower juniors, and can be made into a competition – first pair to touch three lines and so on.

b Move the hoop round the body a number of times, starting by standing in it.

c Spinning activities:

• spin the hoop on the spot and run round it as many times as possible before it 'dies'

• spin it and see if the child can touch one or two lines, for example at opposite sides of the hall/playground, and return to grasp it before it 'dies'.

d Running. Two or three children inside a hoop aim to touch lines and run round a number of obstacles.

Relays
Three children in each team.

i Three hoops are placed close together in a line. Jump, hop or bunny jump into each and round a marker at the back of the team. Touch the next to go.

ii All three stand or sit in line. One hoop is passed back, with each child getting through it.

iii Three hoops in line. Each child has to get through each hoop in order as quickly as possible.

iv **A** and **B** sit in line. **C** moves forward and holds two hoops one at each side, vertically touching the floor. On the signal **A** and **B** run forward, each getting through one of the hoops. They each then take a hoop and place them together in parallel with the ground and leaving a gap of about 35–50cms. **C** moves underneath and gets through. All three sit down back to back with legs outstretched, and pull the two hoops over their heads down onto their thighs.

v As for **iv** but continuous. After touching the thighs the hoop is lifted to stretch height above the head. **A** then jumps up, runs over **B** and **C**'s legs, takes the two hoops and sets them up as described in **iv**. The whole process is repeated twice with **B** setting up the hoops on the last occasion.

Balance
Can be done individually or in pairs.

● with the hoop on the floor. First to balance on the floor in the hoop or on it wins.

● with the hoop off the floor. First to balance with it in contact with specified body parts, or holding it, wins.

Canes

Canes can be used as barriers in a similar way to hoops, in many cases making the activities much easier. They are not, however, recommended as floor targets to move over as they tend to roll or slide when landed on, causing accidents.

a The cane may be positioned at different heights on skittles, or, for whole class work, quick adjustment or more precise positioning, held in the hand by a partner or group member.

● jump over it in different ways

● move over it using other body parts, eg hands; rolling

● roll or slide under it.

It is vitally important from a safety angle that, when a cane is placed in the crimped grooves of modern activity skittles, the child always approaches from the correct direction, that is, from the opposite side to where the cane is placed.

b A series of canes laid on or slotted into the grooves of skittles may be placed in an equally spaced line. Each may be jumped in turn or moved under as in a mini obstacle course.

c In conjunction with a balance bar or bench rib. The cane is held parallel to the floor above the bar. The children move over or under it as for hoops (**8d** *i* and *vii*), the height being adjusted as required.

d Tied to skittles or posts. Canes should never be used for jumping over if tied to posts. Use them for:

● rolling, hitting and kicking balls under

● bouncing balls under or over

● as small goals in attack orientated practices and games.

Lesson structure

1 Whole class

All the class work with the same piece of apparatus at the same time. The teacher sets a number of tasks, or different objectives within a task, and helps the children to attain the highest possible performance levels.

The same apparatus may be used throughout the whole of a lesson and this is advisable in the case of very young children and those who are experiencing a piece for the first time, regardless of age. Variety can be achieved within this system by using two pieces of equipment, possibly revising some work already attempted with the first, and introducing new skills with the second. A few minutes of games that do not require any apparatus could be included at the end of the lesson.

2 Half class

If there is a shortage of some types of apparatus, or the teacher wishes to let some pupils have further experience on one piece while helping lower ability pupils with another, it is possible to use this approach. The relatively unsupervised group must have had previous experience of the piece to be used and be familiar with the task(s) to be attempted. The groups may or may not swap over, depending on what is being attempted and the time available for the lesson or section of the lesson devoted to this activity. It is also possible, if much less frequently done, to divide the class into thirds or a one third/two thirds split, thus allowing the teacher even more contact with selected pupils.

3 Groupwork

Working in thirds as above is the beginnings of groupwork, an excellent lesson format for top infants upwards. Ultimately group numbers may be as small as four; this is ideal for attempting many of the activities included in such a programme in pairs.

Providing there has been a thorough grounding in small apparatus work, the groupwork system can provide for as many as eight or nine activities to be operating at the same time and enable groups of different ability levels to work in parallel. Activities can involve:

- further practice at skills attempted in larger groups

- exploring new uses, including at middle and upper junior level the very rewarding making up of games and relays with certain designated pieces of equipment (*see Appendix 3*)

- target type, where scores are counted and attempts made to improve

- dribbling activities

- specific game practices and games themselves which may be run in parallel with the other types of groupwork.

It may be advisable to move up gradually towards larger numbers of groups, starting at three or four, and adding one activity at a time.

Junior pupils may be grouped according to ability, and the form or condition of the activity changed to match that ability, for example one hand instead of two in catching activities, the difficulty of the balance tasks on the bench and the distance between the objects in a dribbling circuit.

In the early stages of developing groupwork, where tasks are simple and/or there are a small number of groups, all activities may be attempted in one lesson. Later, depending on experience, complexity and time, as few as three may be attempted, with pupils moving on to the next activity in the next lesson or moving in the reverse direction from a standard starting point. Covering four sets in an eight group layout is a reasonable minimum aim; the remaining sets can be worked on in the following lesson.

A major advantage of this system is that it gives all pupils an opportunity to use certain items of equipment which are normally only present in small numbers and could never be employed in a whole class, same-activity lesson; for example high or low wooden posts designed for use with nets, series of cones/skittles for dribbling round, cricket stumps or small goals (real or painted on walls), concentric circles on a wall and benches used for balance work, or as low 'nets'.

The following examples of activity lay-outs cater for classes of up to 36 children if there are four in each group. Changes can be made to cater more precisely for particular levels of ability, numbers, space and equipment.

Activity lay-outs

Example 1

Suitable for middle and top infants.

Divide the class into four to six groups and work on activities already covered in class work, eg moving over a beanbag or rope, moving round or into a hoop, rolling or bouncing a ball, throwing/catching a beanbag, throwing the bag over lines or into a hoop and balancing on the beanbag, or on and in hoops.

Example 2

Suitable for top infants and lower juniors.
Activity 1

A net is suspended as shown across two stands. A medium or large sized ball is rolled or kicked between the posts and under the net, the children operating in two pairs. Alternatively the ball may be thrown over the net to bounce and be caught or to land in a marked area using painted or chalked lines.
Activity 2

Two pairs of ropes are laid down as shown. Pupils aim to move over them.
Activity 3
Pupils stand in pairs a short distance apart and pass a ball or beanbag. The actual task would depend on past experience and group (or pair) capability. For example, catching in a variety of ways, possibly moving further apart with success, rolling or bouncing a ball using one or two hands, kicking and so on.
Activity 4
Pupils (again in pairs) aim to roll, bounce or kick a ball, which may vary in size according to ability, between two cones. The distance between the markers and between the partners can be varied according to task difficulty and pupil skill levels.
Activity 5
Four cones or markers are placed in square or rectangular formation. The children steer or dribble a ball, normally fairly large at this stage, round the obstacles. They may use hands to roll the ball, aiming initially to keep contact with it, or they may use sticks or feet, moving clockwise and anti-clockwise.
Activity 6
Two pairs have ten beanbags each or per pair and aim to throw as many as possible into a container. Pupils can concentrate on improving their own score, can add their scores together and aim to improve as a pair or can compete against each other. Different distances, forms of throwing and either hand or two hands together can be used.

60

Activity 7
For this activity use a bench in a normal upright position plus beanbags and/or hoops. Pupils aim to move along the bench while balancing a bag; throwing it to self or partner; picking it up, or getting through or in and out of the hoop. Spare beanbags or hoops can be used for balancing by one pair while the other works on the bench. Alternatively two benches may be used.

Activity 8
Three pupils stand outside a marked circle (3–4 metres in diameter) and, using a medium or large sized ball, aim to hit the legs of the fourth child who is standing inside the circle: 'solo dodge ball'. Pupils may be encouraged to roll, bounce or throw the ball at the legs.

Activity 9
A large sized hoop is placed centrally between two off-set pairs as shown. One partner aims to bounce a ball in the hoop for the other to catch it on the other side. Non preferred hands can be used and distances adjusted as skill improves.

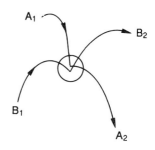

Example 3

Suitable for middle and, with some variations, top juniors.
Activity 1
A net is suspended across two stands and normally there is a marked court, either painted or chalked in lines on the playground.

Two pairs, working separately at first, throw a medium/large sized ball over the net **a** to each other, **b** to a space to force the partner to run for it – ensuring alternate attempts for safety and **c** to try to hit targets such as hoops or skittles. Pairs may also combine to play the game of Newcomb, in which the object is either to get the ball to bounce on court on the opponents' side of the net, or to force the opponents, by quick and accurate throwing to space or faking direction, to drop the ball. Throws must be taken from where the ball is caught and no jumping is allowed. The net must be at least the full stretch height of the tallest player, or if it is lower, no throws aimed in a downward direction are allowed.

Activity 2
Three markers are placed in triangular formation 3 to 4 metres apart and the children skip round the circuit. This is normally a progression from class based work where tight corners have not been negotiated.

Activity 3
As for Activity 7 in Example 2, only now the bench is on its back and the rib should be used for the balance work.

Activity 4
By placing markers in a straight line the dribbling circuit can be made much more difficult. Pupils dribble in and out as

shown or, having rounded the end obstacle, return in a staight line as quickly as possible to stop the ball in a marked circle. The circuit can be made more demanding by decreasing the distance between the obstacles or placing restrictions on how the feet or hands may be used. Pupils again work in pairs, with one partner given the opportunity of timing the other using a large faced stop-clock or a stop-watch. Aiming to improve on a recorded time is an excellent incentive.

Activity 5

'Tower ball.' In this game the three on the outside of a circle aim to knock down a skittle placed in the centre. The player in the centre tries to protect the skittle but is not allowed to touch it.

Activity 6

Using flat bats the children hit a ball across a low net or bench in pairs. The pairs work separately at first, aiming to keep the ball going. When competent the pairs can combine and aim to keep the ball going between them. As skill improves a small court can be used and a game played. It is worthwhile to let the children create their own rules.

Activity 7

Wall targets – these may be concentric circles or squares and rectangles. Pupils aim balls of different sizes at the target: throwing, bouncing, kicking with a bounce and from the floor, flicking, heading or scooping up with a stick. Partners may provide throws for heading and ground passes for kicks.

Activity 8

Make up a game or relay, for example with **a** a flat bat, an airflow ball and two hoops or **b** two ropes and six beanbags (*see Appendix 3*).

Activity 9

Three pupils have possession of a ball, beanbag or quoit and must inter-pass without running with it. The remaining group member attempts to intercept. If the three are too adept conditions may be introduced, such as a restricted area, no passes above head height, a time limit on holding the object, only pass to a person on the move and so on. This activity is an example of a practice that could be used as part of a passing game development programme.

Many other activities can be drawn from the apparatus units, plus small side passing or solo hitting games. Additionally, some activities can be changed by using a different piece of equipment, eg a rugby ball instead of a round ball.

4 Free choice

Pupils may be given the opportunity to choose a piece of apparatus themselves and work with it for given lengths of time, say five minutes. A case can be made for allowing the children this choice at an early stage in the development, but as children at this stage do not tend to respond with an imaginative range of uses but to concentrate on the obvious, even when not always suitable, it is normally better that such a choice should be allowed after a thorough grounding in each piece of apparatus has been given. The children may then consolidate, try to master a previously attempted technique, move a stage further or attempt something new.

An excellent example of this type of development was afforded by two ten-year-old Liverpool girls, who began within a prescribed class activity and developed a six movement synchronised skipping sequence. Over a period of two to three months, and working solely within the five minute period at the start of each lesson allowed for free choice, they built up the sequence to thirteen ways, all different and all perfectly joined and synchronised. This was an outstanding achievement, on a par with the best gymnastic sequences that primary children can produce.

Types of lesson: summary

1 Whole class working on normally one, or sometimes two, pieces of equipment.

2 Half class works on one piece, half class on another (with or without swapping over).

3 Groupwork throughout a whole lesson.

4 As for 1, 2 or 3 but in addition allowing a free choice of apparatus for a period of time, normally at the beginning.

5 Part of the lesson on whole class work, part on groupwork.

6 Part of the lesson on whole class or groupwork, part on simple games/relays.

7 Part of the lesson on small apparatus work, part on major game practices or small side team games.

The time available would dictate whether a particular lesson form is used.

Progression

It is vitally important that different activities are repeated many times over a fairly wide time span, either with the whole class or possibly in groups, to allow all pupils to practice when maturation and experience levels create the best potential for showing improvement or complete mastery.

In general the challenge to the pupils would be increased not only as they grow older and thus exhibit improved potential, but as they actually demonstrate improved competence and a desire to move on. The challenge may take the form of improving an already attempted and possibly half mastered skill, attempting more difficult variations of a skill, eg one handed catching or jumping to catch, increasing the range of activities attempted and being involved in more complex tasks, possibly requiring larger numbers and/or more complicated organisation. Most important however, is that with progression tasks should be geared more specifically to individual levels of attainment and need – either within a whole class situation or in groups.

Young infants should always work as a whole class; middle-top infants will normally do so, with provision for a bigger range of possible answers or levels of skill in a given task, for example catching at different heights, or balancing the beanbag on different parts while moving, and sometimes engaging in simple groupwork.

Lower to middle junior work would depend initially on whether a comprehensive programme had been attempted in the previous years. A lot of basic whole class work would be required if little had been attempted in the past, since the simpler skills contribute to a 'platform' upon which more complex skills are built. Some would be essential, whatever the experience, but the trend would be towards more group activity, more opportunities for choice, some opportunities to make up games (*see Appendix 3*) and mixed lessons including ball games and skills, particularly as they move towards the upper end of the school.

Upper juniors, providing that basic practice in small apparatus work had been undertaken in previous years, would concentrate more on the groupwork and specific major game skill orientated lessons.

Time allocation

The time given to different aspects of PE would be dependent on a number of factors, including facilities and their availability (particularly the hall but also playground size and whether a field is available), the total time given to PE and whether the class goes swimming or not and, of great importance, the enthusiasms and competence of the staff. If, for example, a particular member of staff has great knowledge of and interest in a particular area it would be foolish not to allow ample time for standards to be achieved within it. The following discussion assumes such flexibility and the suggestions on timetabling are in no way intended to be binding.

Infants

Assuming four or five lessons per week of 15–30 minutes in length.

In parallel with for example, one movement to music, one dance/movement or dance drama and one to two gymnastics/ movement lessons per week, it might be expected that at the lower end one period of small apparatus work (including gymnastic type skills) would run throughout the year. This allocation may possibly increase to two periods a week in the summer term of the first year, taking advantage of both the warmer weather for outdoor work and improved competency. As the pupils mature and become capable of improving skills like catching and throwing they reach a point at the top end of the infants, and continued into the juniors, where work of this sort is even more beneficial and two lessons may be allowed for a larger proportion of the year, if not the whole of it.

Juniors

Assuming an increase in lesson length to 30–40 minutes but a reduction in the number given to PE to three.

Again it would make a lot of sense at the lower end to continue to stress basic skills (not major games), introducing a little more competition and a number of 'small' games and to give a similar percentage of the time available as that enjoyed by the top infants. The breakdown could be different however, for example two lessons per week right through the summer term and halfway through the autumn term, one per week for the remainder of that term and none in the spring term. If hall demands made such an ideal breakdown impossible then one period per week throughout the year plus an extra one for part of the summer would suffice.

In the middle juniors, although the percentage of time given to work with these pieces of apparatus may remain the same, it would be expected that there would be a move towards aspects of major games techniques, small group competitive practices, eg 'overload' as in three against one, and games. It is vital that basic skills using beanbags, balls, bats and so on are still included in the programme and that all the lessons do not become, say, football or netball, particularly if a major proportion of the time is taken up with playing games with full sized teams. At this stage however, the moving over/ through and balancing on/with activities should be included in the gymnastics lessons.

In the top juniors, particularly where the children have already experienced a comprehensive small apparatus skills programme, the trend would be further towards games as such, with a bigger total amount of time given to a range of skills practices and actual games (the main stress in the invasion type would be on small sided versions, eg 4 versus 4). Some of these practices and related games can be included in groupwork lessons.

The table below gives a rough guide to a percentage breakdown of time allocated to PE, with swimming omitted.

	Infants		Juniors		
	Lower	Upper	Lower	Middle	Upper
Movement/Music	20	} 30	–	–	–
Dance etc.	20		20	20	} 50
Gymnastics	30	30	40	40	
Small Apparatus	30	40	40	} 40	} 50
Games – Specific	–	–	–		

Strategies and teaching points

1 There is scope for using a variety of strategies in teaching the material, including exploration – where children are encouraged to discover for themselves, possibly with one or two pointers from the teacher – and limitation type tasks but the main approach, particularly in the early stages, should be directed teaching, either where the children do exactly what the teacher tells or shows them, or work within a narrow range of alternatives on a specified activity.

2 Teachers should aim to demonstrate as much as possible, either themselves or via children, and hopefully aim to use as many of the children in the class as possible over a given period of time. Demonstrations can be given before the activity is done and at different stages of a skill's development (*see* **3**).

3 Allow pupils to practice and become familiar with the spatial orientation and nature of an activity before stressing more technical aspects, eg position of feet/hands or how to pass the ball, otherwise there is too much to take in at once. A second demonstration is most useful at this stage.

4 Aim to show as much as possible of how an activity operates, either prior to or in parallel to explanations, which should be kept brief. Check back for understanding.

5 Checking to see if pupils are actually doing what is required and producing the expected result can be done by either simply observing the class at work or, particularly, where a range of different answers are expected: **a** random selection of individuals to show the rest of the class, or **b** having half the class demonstrate while the other half observe, ideally using the 'register' technique. This is where they are instructed to watch the child whose name is nearest to their own in the register, thus ensuring that they do not select the nearest or the best or attempt to watch more than one pupil at a time. Observation in some instances may be aided by pointing out what to look for in advance.

6 Question and answer may be used, with selected demonstrations or checks, to help establish the response to a task (where the children act as the teacher's eyes), to improve powers of observation and to aid in establishing criteria which will help the children to understand what is being aimed for and assess their own performances.

7 Encouragement can be of great value – particularly for infants.

8 Praise is essential but must only be given when it has been earned. It is essential that reasons are given for the praise, ie as reinforcement, for example 'Well done David, you really stretched when you jumped and caught the ball', 'Very good, Amanda, you were just like a statue when you balanced on the hoop – really still'. Other pupils hear and aim to do the same themselves.

9 Feedback is essential. The pupils must be informed of how they have been getting on – en masse and, as often as possible, individually. Motivation is dependent on it and partly because of this and partly because information is required for skills development to take place, there will be little or no progress without it. Aim to be positive, ie stressing what is right and how a skill can be improved further by concentrating on particular points, as opposed to being negative – stressing what has gone wrong. When feedback is given it is advisable that the children should have an opportunity of working immediately afterwards to act on what is said while it is fresh in mind. If this is not possible it may make sense to save the 'constructive' elements, ie those which stress what needs to be done, until there is an opportunity to work on them – the following small apparatus lesson, for example.

10 Background comments, called out as the children work, can be very helpful in suggesting ideas, clarifying or simply reiterating the task, or in stressing what to aim for in a technique.

To summarise, in order to achieve the best possible results it is essential that each child should be as motivated as possible, should have a clear idea of what he/she is trying to do (with tasks geared to ability levels and needs), can operate safely and should have ample time for guided practice. The children should receive some form of feedback as an aid to knowing how well a task was done and what needs stressing; this will lead to further learning and to increased motivation.

Storage of equipment

Small items of equipment, for example beanbags, quoits and ropes, are best kept in light wire baskets. Ideally these can be stored on small, wheeled trolleys; models are available to stack three baskets of adequate size or, more expensive, four with a larger capacity and an attachment for hoops. Alternatively each basket can be stored, neatly and separately, on shelves or on the floor against a wall in a storeroom designed or designated for this purpose. Where this facility does not exist the baskets may either be stored in corners or against the wall in the hall, providing it is safe to leave them there. If there is some danger of the equipment being tampered with or tripped over, baskets should be kept in storerooms in other parts of the school, the apparatus being rolled or carried to each lesson as required.

Sacks or nets may be used for medium and large sized balls and these can be placed in the storerooms either on the floor, if there is plenty of room, or suspended from hooks.

Hoops may be tied with braid in sets according to size, type, number or weight. These in turn may be suspended from hooks or nails placed in the wall or shelving in a storeroom or hall. Actual positioning and number of hoops in a set would depend on who was expected to carry them – a teacher, or pupils of different ages. Permanent stands with 'arms' on which the hoops are placed may also be used but, as there is a tendency for many models to be unstable, it may be advisable to secure them to a wall or post to avoid accidents. Braids, in sets of colours tied up with a differently coloured band, may also be hung from pegs or nails.

Sectioned rectangular wire baskets are ideal in that a number of each piece of small apparatus can be placed in each section. Depending on class numbers, class groups (normally four, each given a colour) can be instructed to collect whatever piece is required from the appropriate basket, often marked by a piece of braid – matching the team/group colour – and placed in different sections of the hall. Contents could be 8–10 beanbags, 8–10 small balls, 8–10 ropes, 4 or 5 quoits, 4 or 5 airflow balls, 4 flat bats and 10 braids. Additional pieces could be stored separately if required for the whole class, eg a flat bat each.

Cones, skittles and posts should be stacked neatly together against a wall in the storeroom **or** out of the hall **or** in a cordoned off section of the hall – never simply standing where contact may be made with them during the course of a lesson.

Distribution of equipment

1 Pupils in their designated teams line up in single file at the appropriate basket, placed at least two metres from a wall, and take one each of the required item(s).

2 Where all items of a particular piece of apparatus are stored in one container or, for example in the case of hoops, are permanently stored in a given position, pupils line up in single file and take one each, normally under the direct supervision of the teacher. According to instructions the pupils

• will begin work immediately if the practice has already been explained and demonstrated and the teacher is observing the class to check on spacing

• will hold the piece of equipment

• will place the piece on the floor so that there is no longer any contact with it.

3 When working in small groups, particularly if on sets of different types of apparatus, it is best to organise the pupils with regard to numbers, space and position before one from each group, or all team members, collect the equipment.

4 Pupils should not be allowed a choice of apparatus from different points until it is ensured that all can line up sensibly and patiently wait their turn.

5 When the apparatus is no longer required it is carried to its container or storage point and placed carefully in position. It is never thrown or rolled.

Pupil organisation

1 Free spacing

As much space as possible is left between each pupil. Weather permitting, the children should sit down in their spaces when required to observe others working and normally when listening to instructions.

2 Pairs

Pupils would normally be expected to select their own partners and when they have done so to sit down, or crouch if the playground is damp. This is a quick, simple method which stops children transferring from one pair to another and makes it very easy for both children and teacher to see who has not yet got a partner. As pupils of like ability tend to go together they are usually well matched in respect of task difficulty.

3 Groups

a If the standard in each group doesn't matter the pupils can form their own groups either from scratch, or, if multiples of two are required in each set, by combining pairs. Alternatively the teacher can randomly or deliberately select groups depending on whether some form of balance is wanted, eg between the sexes, or if certain pupils are being kept apart.

b When groupwork is to be based on ability, with different conditions being imposed (eg form or time limit on passing) or different tasks being used according to standard, then the teacher could pre-select the groups before the lesson or, mindful of the problems caused to such a system by absentees, attempt to put the pupils into graded groups during the lesson. As this can be time consuming and not always totally accurate it may be advisable to use a variant of method **a**. Allow the children to form their own groups of, say, four. For a variety of reasons, pupils of like ability tend to go together; the teacher can then decide on the capability level of each group. Alternatively, have the pupils line up in a double column of pairs down the hall as shown.

a_1	b_1	c_1	d_1	e_1	f_1	g_1	h_1
a_2	b_2	c_2	d_2	e_2	f_2	g_2	h_2

As more skillful and confident pupils tend to come to the front, it is a simple matter to split off the first two pairs and designate them **group 1** (a_1, a_2, b_1, b_2) and so on down the line.

If the groups are to be permanent the pupils respond well to team names, eg animals (Antelopes, Bears or Cats) or birds.

In all cases the teacher demonstrates what spacing is required.

4 Teams

Selecting teams of equal ability to play each other has long been a problem in games lessons. The most efficient way in terms of both matching and speed is to have the pupils line up in a double column of matched pairs as shown in **3** above. The teacher splits the line at an appropriate point, depending on how many are required in a team; for example, in a game comprising five per side a_1, b_1, c_1, d_1, e_1 play a_2, b_2, c_2, d_2, e_2. Stronger performers play together and each can be expected to play a full part, something that tends not to happen if weak players are integrated with the strong. Similarly pupils of average and poorer ability levels also play together and have better opportunities of expressing themselves within the game. If the whole class is to be divided into two equal teams then all those on the teacher's right play all those on the teacher's left.

There is one method of selection that should **never** be used: that of pupils acting as captains and 'picking' the remaining class members in turn. Not only does it often result in imbalanced teams, but it can be most painful for the less competent – already only too aware of their status – who are selected last.

5 Relays

It is very difficult to produce teams of exactly equal ability so that all have a chance of winning. It is, however, vital that the attempt is made. Random picking or pupil self-selection will not work and the teacher must

a aim to create a series of balanced teams, say, one known good performer, two of average ability, possibly one just above and one just below, and one poor in a team of four

b make adjustments as necessary as the competitions take place.

In pairs relays everyone can be given new partners quite simply by moving the whole of the 'front line' one place down the hall, with the very end pupil who no longer has a partner moving to the opposite end.

Numbers in teams should be kept as small as possible to allow for maximum participation by each individual. Twos or possibly threes are ideal where movement is one at a time, with one child moving across a section of floor and returning to the team base. Where objects are passed down a line in some way three or, at the most, four are ideal. Aim to avoid at all costs the traditional format of teams of six or more, where one child is moving while the remaining five or more stand or sit. Children of this age have an enormous capacity to keep moving and should have opportunities to repeat a relay once it is understood. This can be done quickly and often if teams are kept small. Waiting long periods for a turn is not acceptable (*see Safety considerations and Appendix 3*).

Judging competitions

1 Individuals or pairs – working on the spot

The teacher should stand in the corner of the hall or playground. The pupils should sit or crouch down on the completion of the activity. This is much clearer than raising hands although this time honoured technique can be employed if the pupils are already sitting at the end of the competition.

2 Individuals, pairs or teams – moving across a given distance

a Where there is no common starting or finishing position the teacher again stands in the corner with all pupils sitting down and, in the case of pairs and teams, one child raises a hand. In situations where the pupils work sequentially this would be the last to finish, in other cases a designated leader.

b Where teams are lined up in parallel **i** in cases where individuals or teams working together cross a line the teacher must stand at the end of the line; **ii** in cases where objects are passed down a line, or team members move and return to a given point, the last members of each team should be in line with each other. The teacher stands not quite in line but slightly off-set, in order to be able to see when each team finishes. As above the teams would either sit down or raise hands as appropriate.

Safety considerations

1 Surfaces

All surfaces to be used must be in a safe condition. Playgrounds and particularly fields should be checked for anything that may cause injury, for example glass or tins. Surfaces must be in good condition: no holes, loose gravel or splintered wood. Hall floors should be clean and dry. Wet surfaces indoors can be lethal and pupils should never be allowed access until a floor is completely dry. Any section that is still wet when the floor is in use should be cordoned off; it is not enough for pupils to be told to avoid such areas.

2 Distances

Activities must take place a safe distance from doors, windows, walls, portable objects such as gymnastic apparatus and anything that juts out dangerously towards the space being used; for complete safety the latter may have to be covered in padding. Particular care must be taken when running activities and chasing games are taking place.

3 Relays

Children must not run to solid objects, such as walls, as turning or finishing points in races. It is essential that pupils either turn round a small safe object designed partly for this purpose, such as a cone, skittle or even a beanbag, or run and touch with hand, foot or finger a marked line or suitable object such as a skipping rope or, again, a beanbag.

Where races finish by moving across a prescribed line, sufficient distance must be allowed beyond the line for all participants to pull up comfortably short of any solid or dangerous portable object. The actual distance will vary according to the nature of the race and form of movement.

Plenty of room, a minimum of 2 metres, should be left between teams competing in parallel.

4 Equipment

a Pieces of equipment no longer being used should not be left lying about or even placed at the side of the actual area being used; they are potential hazards and can easily lead to broken bones or bruising. All equipment must be put away in the proper receptacle, never simply thrown or rolled in the general direction of the container.

b Only safe objects must be used as markers: cones, beanbags or plastic shapes designed for this purpose, never cricket stumps or chairs.

c All equipment should be checked regularly for wear and tear, for example splinters on wooden hoops and skittles or bat handles coming loose.

d Specific points concerning particular pieces of equipment or practices are made in the activity units: some are absolutely vital:

• Common sense would dictate that balls of the medium to hard type are never thrown, kicked or hit wildly and particularly so near windows or roads

• Hitting implements should not be released after hitting a ball, but should be carried when runs are scored. Most children will put them down in a specified place but unfortunately a minority throw them, creating hazardous situations

• Objects to be jumped, such as canes, should never be held by more than one person, tied to posts or placed at the wrong (ie near) side of skittles or posts. Pupils should not jump them in the 'wrong' (ie reverse) direction.

5 Pupils

Kit
Different types of kit may be worn according to season, indoor/outdoor activity or school rules, and may include

• shorts, games skirts, knickers or underpants plus T shirt, blouse or sports shirt

• tracksuits

• jumpers in cold conditions

• bare feet (where floors are both clean and dry), gymshoes or trainers.

On no account should

• shoes or plastic sandals (ie with shiny soles) be worn

• indoor work be done in stockinged feet

• any activity be attempted with cardigan or tracksuit top hanging open, or in dresses or long trousers.

Jewellery
All medallions, badges, earrings, bracelets, rings, watches and everything other than the required clothes should be removed and kept in a safe place.

Task limits
Pupils should always know exactly what they have to do and the limits to the area(s) they can operate in.

6 Teacher

Teachers should

• have full knowledge of pupils' health and fitness to participate

• never leave the class unattended

• have full knowledge of safety points regarding all equipment and each activity

- keep checking to see that pupils are working within imposed limits

- keep checking to see that pupils are using the apparatus in the correct way and that none has been left lying in a dangerous position

- know what to do in case of accident.

Further information on safety can be found in the definitive (DES approved) *Safe Practice in Physical Education* published by BAALPE (British Association of Advisers and Lecturers in Physical Education) and available from
    White Line Press
    60 Bradford Road
    Stanningley
    Leeds LS28 6EF.

Pupils

It is vital that information on the results of a programme is collected and that this information is in turn linked to an evaluation of the effectiveness of the material used and the teaching and organisational skills employed. Immediate planning and more long term projections can then be based on the class, group and individual needs ascertained.

It is of great value if a record of class and/or individual attainments, along with the material and practices covered, can be kept in a file and passed on through the school from teacher to teacher.

Assessment may be based entirely on objective information or may make reference to 'quality' in execution, or even specific aspects of a technique or skill ('sub-skills').

To take catching a beanbag or small ball as an example, the different levels of assessment may be as follows:

1 How many of the class can catch it in two hands? (eg when thrown individually a specified distance above the head, or when thrown by a partner standing 3 or 4 metres away)

If the answer is 17 out of 30 on a given attempt it might be assumed that 13 need further practice and that the 17 could move on to greater distances, or different levels.

But

2 How often is the object caught? How 'well' is the ball caught?

An assessment of how often the ball is caught as a percentage of the number of attempts made and, even better, the facility with which it is caught (that is movement, positioning, use of hands and arms) can indicate more precisely just who needs practice in order to perfect the skill.

By awarding a simple scoring scale to each person's attempts a more accurate picture of class ability may be gained.

For example,

3 points   Catches it 90–100% and/or

Adjusts feet quickly and well; moves arms in exactly the right way

2 points   Catches it 60–90%

Some movement but at times hesitant; hands in right position but not pulled in

1 point   Catches it 20–60%

Rarely if ever moves feet; arms held rigid

Immediately the picture becomes much clearer. Threes are clearly capable of moving on and would benefit from practices involving greater movement, more difficult positioning or one hand only. Twos need a mixture of practices replicating the tested skill and some new slightly more difficult ones. Ones, and possibly Twos for part of the time, need practices that draw attention in a positive way to the aspects of the technique that need improvement. Some Ones, and any failing to score 20% (including those too poor to be exposed to the test) need very basic practices at lower heights or shorter distances, such as tossing gently into double cupped hands from close range. They should wait a while until maturation levels allow practice at the original distance or height to be productive. As stated earlier, equal capability must never be assumed.

A record of achievement may best be kept by using a class profiling sheet as shown.

Name	Skills											
	1				2				3			
	0	1	2	3	0	1	2	3	0	1	2	3
Brown, James		✓										
Brunning, Amanda			✓									
Carter, Jane		✓	✓									
Corbyn, Fred	✓											
Dalton, Jenny			✓									
Emery, Charles		✓	✓									
Fawzi, Mohammed			✓									
Fletcher, Merlene		✓		✓								

Date (1) ✓   9. 9.99
Date (2) ✓   4.11.99

An attached list indicates what a particular numbered skill is. Underneath a record of the dates when assessments were made can be kept, and different coloured inks used to show at a glance when a standard was achieved. Duplicated sheets can be used for the whole school, with only the names and year to be filled in.

The teacher has now begun to make a subjective evaluation and can analyse to a degree the reasons why a pupil may or may not be skillful. This is most useful since, although practice per se may have a little value, practice in which the children are asked to concentrate on particular facets of a skill is far more productive. It may be possible from current observation or memory to know what aspect to concentrate on with a given child, but if desired a separate sheet for one skill can be used, with short notes beside each name or ticks and crosses in columns headed with features of the technique.

It is also helpful to develop a separate profile for each pupil, with sections for each aspect of physical education including, at infant and lower junior level, one for basic skills using small apparatus. Each skill could be given a score reflecting the current ability level or a tick when mastered. Ongoing needs can be identified and noted and either a short termly or annual report written under the assessment scores.

Assessment should never become the tail that wags the dog, however. Periods of time may be allocated, say every fourth lesson, with five to ten minutes spent assessing the whole class on a specific skill; pupils may record their own or a partner's score out of ten or, when capable, report back on a facet of a movement that they have been asked to focus on – something which in the long term helps to improve understanding and execution of a skill. Alternatively observe a more limited number in more depth, say five or six, concentrating on one at a time.

Teachers

Teachers can usefully analyse their own performance – the most vital factor in improving pupil skill – by evaluating both lesson content and teaching. Time-saving checklists can be used and are best filled in on the day that the lesson was taught. Use ticks or symbols to record whether an aspect was satisfactory or required attention, or written comments with reflections on reasons for this. The checklist or comments can be looked at when planning the next lesson.

Aspects that may be included on a checksheet and/or referred to in other forms of evaluation are listed below:

Lesson/programme and teaching evaluation

Organisation

Availability, distribution and collection of apparatus
Pupils – setting up groups etc.

Material

Task suitability. Timing and length of task. The balance of the material, both in one lesson and over a period of time.

There is a need for both familiarity through repetition and variety, the balance depending on maturation and skill level.

There has to be sufficient practice to allow feedback to take effect and improvement to occur; variety may be achieved via small changes in task structure.

Communication and development skills

Explanations, possibly checking for understanding
Use of voice and gesture
Positioning and movement
Comments – when the pupils are stopped and while they work ('background')
Use of demonstrations
Question and Answer
Encouragement; reinforcement (praise with reasons)
Feedback – the class and individuals
Individual help or coaching
Checking pupil progress – where appropriate

Overall – some key questions

Were the children motivated?

Did they have a clear idea of what they had to do?

Could they operate safely?

Where appropriate did they understand the criteria for success in the task?

Did they have sufficient time for guided practice?

Was feedback given to the class or individuals and was there sufficient time to act on it?

Did most, if not all, the pupils improve in some respect?

Was there some aspect of the lesson that was very successful?

Was there some aspect(s) of the lesson that might be improved in future?

Appendix 1 *Dribbling circuits*

Circuits are designed to test skill at controlling a ball, or occasionally a beanbag or quoit, with hand(s), foot/feet or stick.

They develop from the simple practices described in Unit 2, for example round an obstacle or between two obstacles, and become progressively more difficult through adjustment of lay-out design, spacing, obstacles used and task demand.

The simpler circuit types (**1** and **2** below) may be used by the whole class, with three or four pupils working on each circuit, while all of the types described may be incorporated in groupwork (*see Unit 7*), with choice of form depending on the range of pupil ability.

It must not be assumed, however, that improvement in the technique of dribbling round fixed markers will produce parallel improvement on the field of play. Practice against opponents in some form is essential for this to happen.

1 The easiest circuits to negotiate are those which involve moving round the outside of large regular shapes, with difficulty increasing with the use of angles and their degree of sharpness:

- oval/ellipse

- circle

- square/rectangle

- triangle

2 The pupils then progress to straight line formations, starting with comfortable distances between the markers – say 2 to 3 metres. Difficulty is increased by having to stop and start at given points, possibly hoops, or shortening the distance between the markers.

3 Further demands may then be made on the pupils by introducing:

- variations in both the angles and distances between the markers, allowing or 'forcing' both sharp turns and differences in speed

81

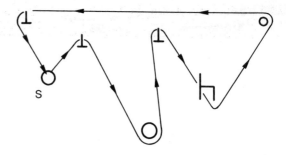

S = start and finish

• at any point, in terms of circuit shape, limitations on which hand or foot can be used

• the pupils may also time themselves in pairs, allowing opportunities for repetition to improve personal scores ('Beat the record'), or small matched pairs competitions with the two pupils in each team adding their scores together. Timing in this way, using a large timing clock or, more accurately, a stop-watch, can also help pupils with their understanding of certain mathematical concepts, for example when they are adding times together.

Golden rule: keep teams as small as possible

Ideal numbers are two to three children, where one child runs or moves at a time, and three to four where objects are passed from one to the next, or where all work together in unison.

Basic – straight line

For safety reasons pupils must not run to a wall or similar large solid object but ideally should run round an obstacle: cones, marker domes and skittles are ideal but beanbags or even quoits will suffice. Failing that, the pupils should touch a marker or line on the ground with hand or foot before returning.

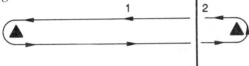

(Starting/Finishing line)

To cut out any unfair advantage, by team members moving out to meet an incoming runner, and to make the activity safer, the relay is organised so that pupils always run past the next stationary competitor and return from behind to touch, or better, pass on an object such as a baton, quoit or beanbag.

Laps – geometric shapes

Each pupil moves round a regular circuit; they could be running, dribbling a ball or balancing an object. Squares or rectangles are ideal as they only require four markers and the angles are not too sharp. On completing a lap each child hands on the object to the next in order, who has taken up the starting position by the first marker.

Circuits – agility or dribbling

Activities as described in Appendix 1 are used as the basis for a relay, with the ball passed on to the next competitor. Transfer can be by making a short pass, or by stopping the ball dead in a circle before the next dribbler can touch it. Or, on completing the circuit, the ball is passed between two markers and, as soon as it is through, the next team member can begin.

'Spry' type

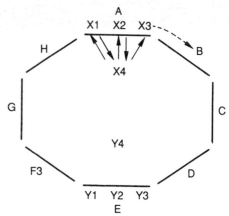

A, B, C, D, E, F, G and H represent an eight team lay-out.

Teams of four or five may, according to skill and availability of equipment, line up as shown in the diagram, standing behind or on a bench, or behind a line marker such as a skipping rope laid on the floor.

Simple version

X4 passes a beanbag, a ball (size depending on age and skill) or a quoit to X1 who returns it. The process is repeated with X2. X4 then passes to X3 who retains it and runs forward to take X4's place. At the same time X4 runs to take X1's place and X1 and X2 shuffle along one place sideways.

The whole process is repeated three times until all have had a turn at the front. Finally, when X4 returns to the centre, all sit down.

Passes may be underarm, overarm or to the chest, and catches two or one handed.

Advanced version

The system is as above until X3 retains the ball. Instead of running to the front X3, followed in order by X2 and X1 and with X4 bringing up the rear, leads the whole team round the back of all the other team positions. On returning to their own bench or marker X3 cuts through the gap to take up the front central position, the other three lining up in order (one space along) behind the bench. The process is repeated until all the pupils have occupied the central position once, and when all the circuits have been completed the team sits down.

It is vital that the pupils stay in the correct order throughout for the relay to work.

Making up games and relays

An excellent way of allowing creativity to flower, and for PE to make a very positive input to the cognitive domain, is to allow pupils to make up their own games and relays.

Providing the children have a platform to work from, that is, a knowledge of the skills and concepts that are required for a given type of activity, even children within the lower intelligence or ability range can produce innovative ideas that work.

Groups of children can all be working on producing a game or relay in one lesson, either all using the same apparatus and area limitations or, so that they may not 'borrow' ideas from neighbours, different sets of apparatus. The pupils may possibly work in groups of different sizes, although no more than six is recommended so that there is a better chance of all making a contribution to the finished product.

Normally group sizes are even, ie four or six, allowing for two teams matched in numbers, and hopefully in ability, to be selected. Occasionally however, odd numbered groups are set up so that games with individual scoring or handicapping must be developed.

For originality it is best to give each group two or three different kinds of apparatus, including markers, rather than one kind only; for example six beanbags and two skipping ropes can be used to produce an excellent range of ideas depending on age, experience with the two pieces and familiarity with the 'process'. The beanbags and ropes in combination naturally lend themselves to relay development and some of the ideas that have been or could be produced are:

a One or more beanbags at a time are transported from behind one rope, acting as a marker line, to behind the other. When all have been moved the next team member carries them back.

b Potato race. The bags are laid out at regular intervals (on painted or chalked spots or lines) in front of each team, who are lined up behind a rope. The first team member runs out and collects any one bag, runs back to the rope, drops it, then goes for the second and third etc. The second team member replaces the bags on the spots or lines.

c Carrying the beanbags on or between parts of the body.

d Part carrying, part skipping.

e Skipping with a beanbag between the feet, perhaps using other bags as markers.

f Balancing and carrying the bag in different ways while skipping.

g As for **e** and **f**, but returning the bag by throwing – the more accurate the throw, the more quickly the next team member can begin skipping.

Other combinations will produce entirely different results, for example one flat bat, one sponge or airflow ball and four skittles will tend to produce a rounders or even cricket type game. One medium or large ball and four cones or hoops, or two of each, give varied opportunities: passing games to hit a target or score a goal, passing and moving competitions and dribbling or steering – one team with the ball, the other undertaking a running task.

Apparatus that is not normally played with outside school can be used to guarantee that something novel will result, for example one quoit, two ropes and two skittles or hoops.

The teacher's role is to prompt thinking by oblique questioning or comment, rather than to give ideas. The right question(s), asked when a game is beginning to take shape or when it is actually being played, can help a great deal in avoiding pitfalls and in refining the game, so that it functions properly and may be tried by the rest of the class. It may also be necessary, particularly when the making up of games is first being tried, to impose certain limitations in order to help the children find worthwhile answers.

To avoid the possibility of copying, when each group in the class is working with different apparatus or each is to attempt one set in a rotating groupwork lesson, no demonstrations are given until all have had their opportunity. This may mean that the children have to record their games via diagrams or lists of rules.

Additional activities

These could include:

- hitting or dribbling a ball with sticks (work in pairs)

- basic bat and ball work (individually or in pairs), possibly to a wall or ground target

- balancing using rope(s) or quoit(s) on the floor, a hoop or a bench

- throwing to hit or knock down a skittle

- competing at target activities, such as wall circles, for accuracy or speed; if in pairs, attempting to keep the ball in play, for example, hitting or kicking a ball to a target alternately with one or two bounces allowed

- solo skipping on the spot

- skipping circuits (as for dribbling – see Appendix 1)

- synchronised skipping

- pairs balance work – particularly with hoops

- different forms of dribbling circuits, including the more advanced 'off-set' variety

- Captain ball. One team member remains in a marked circle, the other three are spaced evenly round the perimeter. The three on the outside aim to inter-pass the ball – below head height – without the player in the centre intercepting it

- French cricket

- net games for top juniors – quoit tennis or badminton

- individual hitting games (see figure)

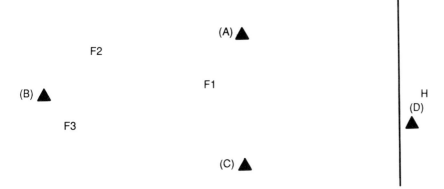

One player, **H**, hits (by throwing up the ball first or receiving a bowled ball) or kicks a ball forwards between two fairly closely-placed markers, **A** and **C**, so that the ball does not interfere with the other activities taking place on the playground or field. **H** then attempts to run round all the markers, **A**, **B** and **C** (as shown), and back to base **D** before fielders **F1**, **F2** and **F3** can retrieve the ball. They either pass it a number of times or roll it through each pair of legs, normally after forming a line. The hitter scores points according to the number of markers passed before the fielders achieve their objective, and normally has three goes for a total score out of twelve before another team member becomes the hitter

- team passing games for top juniors. Two groups would combine for this activity and play four against four (according to ability) at games like pass ball, where they aim to pass the ball a set number of times before the opponents can gain possession, or skittle ball. (NB Working within groups of two against two is very difficult since, with one player in possession, the other team member can effectively be marked by two opponents.)

Many activities may be undertaken with a different piece of apparatus, for example using a rugby ball in games and hand passing practices.

The following lists of apparatus are divided into sections corresponding to age.

Essential refers to what is definitely needed if a comprehensive basic programme, such as is outlined in this book, is to be carried out.

Additional allows for

a expansion – so that all pupils may now use a previously limited piece at the same time

b improving transportation and storage

c apparatus that can help expand the variety in what is available for groupwork, particularly for middle to top juniors.

It is assumed that 40 pieces are sufficient for every child in a large class to have one each and leave some spare as replacements; 20 allow work in pairs and smaller numbers mean that the apparatus would be used in groupwork.

For smaller classes numbers may be reduced proportionally.

Infants

Essential

40 beanbags

40 skipping ropes

40 hoops (20 medium, 10 large, 10 small) – toughened plastic tubing

40 medium sized, light, brightly coloured plastic balls (11–14cms)

20 sponge/foam balls, vinyl coated for outside use; various sizes

10 flat bats – medium size

40 braids

12 marker domes

12 skittles with a serrated edge

Playground chalk

4 large wire baskets – preferably compartmentalised

Nets or sacks for storing the balls

Additional

30 flat bats

20 quoits

2 posts with one long rope or net

1 wheeled trolley, possibly with side structure for storing hoops

6 canes

20 small soft rubber balls

Juniors

Essential

In addition to what is listed under essential for infants

20 large balls (16–18cms)

30 large bats – rectangular

20 quoits

20 airflow balls – small

40 tennis balls or rubber equivalent

10 unihoc sticks

6 canes of 4–6 feet in length

4 sets of 8 to 10 coloured (and preferably numbered) bibs

1 set of posts – badminton size, plus net

4 rugby type plastic balls

8 rounders bats

1 stop clock or watch

1 inflator plus necessary adaptors

16 marker domes or cones (ie making one each with the skittles)

Additional

30 unihoc sticks

20 quoits

1 set of small posts, plus net

additional stopwatches

shuttlecocks

long rope

short tennis racquets or sets of short tennis equipment

badminton posts, plus net

As stated this list refers only to small apparatus and mixed activity groupwork lessons. This and other apparatus may be deemed essential for an actual upper junior games programme.

Suppliers

There are a number of suppliers who stock this type of equipment, some of whom may have links with local LEAs. Two who have an excellent range and can supply everything required are:

Hestair Hope	NES
St Philips Drive	Ludlow Hill Road
Royton	West Bridgford
Oldham	Nottingham
OL2 6AG	NG2 6HD
Telephone: 061 6336611	Telephone: 0602 234251